START EXPLORING™

Places of Mystery

A Fact-Filled Coloring Book

Emmanuel M. Kramer
Illustrated by Helen I. Driggs

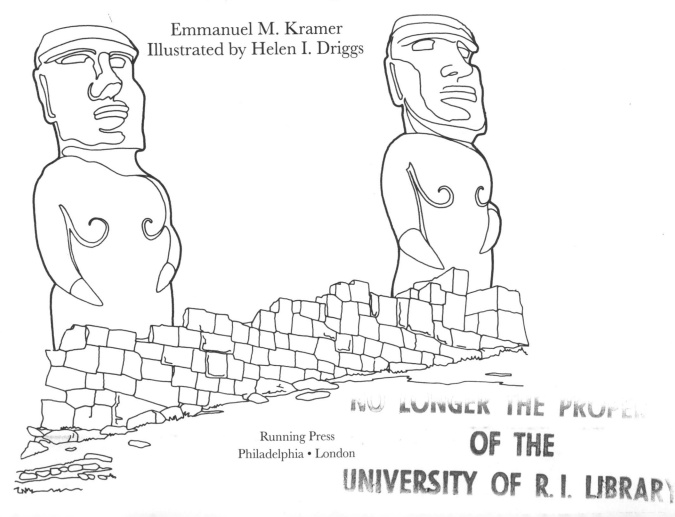

Running Press
Philadelphia • London

Canadian representatives: General Publishing Co., Ltd.,
30 Lesmill Road, Don Mills, Ontario M3B 2T6

9 8 7 6 5 4 3 2 1
Digit on the right indicates the number of this printing.

ISBN 1–56138–193–4

Editorial Director: Nancy Steele
Cover design: E. June Roberts
Interior design: Lili Schwartz
Cover, interior, and poster illustrations: Helen I. Driggs
Illustration on p. 37 based on a photograph by Lee Boltin, copyright © 1976 by Lee Boltin.
Poster copyright © 1994 by Running Press Book Publishers
Typography: Monotype Baskerville by Deborah Lugar
Printed in the United States by Chernay Printing, Inc.

This book may be ordered by mail from the publisher.
Please add $2.50 for postage and handling.
But try your bookstore first!

Running Press Book Publishers
125 South Twenty-second Street
Philadelphia, Pennsylvania 19103-4399

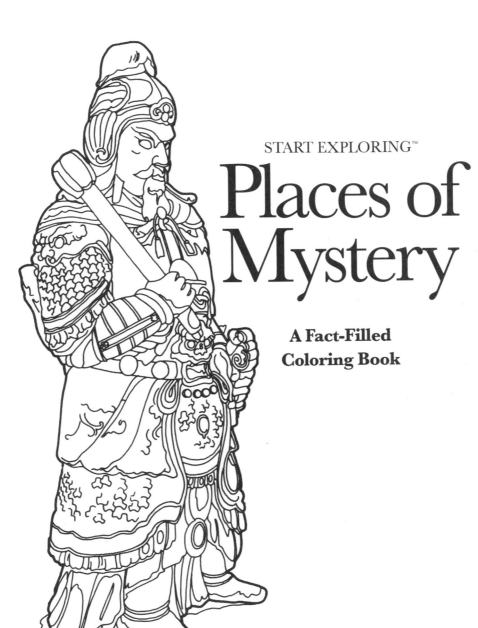

START EXPLORING™

Places of Mystery

A Fact-Filled Coloring Book

Contents

Mysteries of Sacred Places

Mysteries of Natural Wonders

Introduction

The world is filled with mysterious places—natural wonders, prehistoric places, ancient civilizations, and sacred places. Discovering these mysteries helps us better understand ourselves and enriches our understanding of what it means to be a human being.

Natural formations of rocks and mountains, mighty waterfalls, and delicate flowers have inspired our ancestors to create literature, compose songs, and build great works of architecture. The Egyptians wrote poetry about the sun and the Nile River; North American Indians learned to live in harmony with their environment and to adapt to its many forms. The people of ancient Mexico created architectural works that followed the forms suggested by mountains and the height of the jungle canopy.

At Stonehenge, Carnac, and New Grange, we are witness to how early people wondered at the heavens and the great rhythms that silently guide the sun, moon and stars in their daily journey through the endless space of sky. We can observe how these people linked their daily lives to the seasons of the year.

We also witness great hardships. We see the desperation for rain in the Temple of the Thousand Masks in Yucatan, and the brutal working conditions endured by the builders of the Great Wall of China.

Most of all, we witness the triumphs of the human spirit—over unknown fears, over the shocks of earthquakes, floods, and famine, and triumph over the unspeakable cruelty of tyrannical leaders.

From the basic faith of the people of Chimayo to the grandeur of Sainte-Chapelle, the beauty created by many peoples inspires the individual with a sense of hope and purpose for the future of mankind. The places we experience through the pages of this book are evidence of the confidence that the human race has gained while struggling to live in a mysterious universe.

The Caves of Lascaux

The young boys hiking through the fields of a valley in France were searching for the caves of prehistoric people who had lived in the region thousands of years ago. Suddenly, their dog disappeared into a deep hole that had opened where a tree had been uprooted by a recent storm. Following the sound of their barking dog into the hole, the boys quickly realized that they were entering a cave that had been occupied by prehistoric people—but they could not have imagined that they were entering a cave that had been sealed for more than 15,000 years. This discovery, in September of 1940, gave archaeologists an opportunity to study some of the finest examples of prehistoric cave painting ever known.

What the boys saw in the Caves of Lascaux were paintings of horses, reindeer, bison, and cows covering the walls and ceilings.

Many of the animals pictured in the paintings were shown running toward spears that had been placed in their paths. Others seemed to be standing in front of crossed lines that may have represented traps. In some sections of the cave, paintings of animals were placed at points where the natural rock looked like the shape of an animal's head or shoulder.

The play of light and shadow from the torches of the prehistoric painters may have suggested these forms.

Many prehistoric cave sites in France and Spain have pictures of animals painted on their walls, but no one knows why. People may have gathered in these caves to hear stories about animal hunts or to witness ceremonies in which the painted animal figure was "killed" by magic. Perhaps it was believed that killing the image of the animal would bring good luck to the hunt.

It also may be that the cave paintings were part of a celebration of the spring season. Spring plants appear in some of the paintings at Lascaux. Deer are shown holding their heads above water as they cross rivers, perhaps flooded by spring rains. Bison are seen shedding their winter coats, and many of the female animals appear ready to give birth to their offspring.

Winters were very harsh for people living in prehistoric times, and signs of spring must have been most welcome. The ceremonies to announce the arrival of spring that took place among the pictures painted on the walls of the Lascaux caves gave prehistoric people hope—hope that game would be plentiful, the weather would be warm, and the cycle of life would be renewed.

Painted outlines of bison, horses, and other animals can still be seeen after 15,000 years.

The Tomb at New Grange

A mysterious opening appears above the doorway of a large tomb in Ireland where a very important person was buried more than 5,000 years ago. An earthen mound covers the tomb, and the mound is encircled by stones carved with spiral shapes and strange designs. Located at a place called New Grange, the burial mound overlooks a peaceful Irish hillside that offers no hint of the mysterious burial ceremonies associated with this tomb.

Ireland

Inside the tomb is a tunnel leading to three burial chambers. The passageway was made by placing two rows of stones along opposite sides of an aisle. Even larger stones were then placed over the aisle to form a roof that rested on the stones set along the sides of the aisle. The tunnel formed in this way led into burial rooms at the back of the tomb. When all the stonework was finished, it was then enclosed by a huge mound of earth, and the sides of the mound were covered with small stones to hold the earth in place.

The mysterious window-like opening over the entrance to the tomb puzzled archaeologists for many years. Then an interesting discovery was made. On December 21, the shortest day of the year, the rising sun sends a beam of light through the opening over the doorway entrance and down the stone passageway leading to the burial chamber.

In prehistoric times, people became frightened as the days of winter became shorter. They feared that the sun might disappear forever, leaving them in darkness. The window over the door of the tomb had been set to allow the light of the sunrise to enter the passageway of the tomb only on December 21, which marked the shortest day of the year and the time when the days would begin to get longer again. To prehistoric people, this day meant that the sun had been reborn and a new cycle of life had begun.

Perhaps the people who built the tomb at New Grange thought that the light shining along the passageway of the grave site on December 21 would be a signal of rebirth to those buried in the tomb.

Designs like this were often used by the early British people called Celts.

Sheep now graze near the carved stone entrance to an ancient Irish tomb.

The Stones of Carnac

The stone armies of Brittany march across the fields. Three thousand strong, they march along paths chosen for them 5,000 years ago. The mysteries of these large stones, or megaliths, may never be solved.

The thousands of megaliths at Carnac in the Brittany region of France speak of a massive effort in quarrying, transporting, and placing these huge stones in line across a field. What purpose did the stones serve? Who were the people who planned this ambitious project? How did they raise enough food to feed those who labored to set the stones in place? What mathematical knowledge did they have to align the rows of upright stones and measure the circles of smaller stones that were part of the design?

Archaeologists have studied, measured, and excavated megalith sites in France for many years, and still we know very little about the megalith builders of 5,000 years ago.

The people who built these megalithic sites were farmers. They used stone tools, and they developed a religion that the monuments served. The megaliths must have helped them develop a sense of community as they shared the work of building the monuments and as they shared the religious ideas that the monuments represented.

By arranging these huge stones, the farmers may have been practicing early astronomy and developing a calendar. The avenues of stones appear to be sighting points for the solstices measuring the longest and shortest days of the year. To know of the coming of the seasons, when to plant and when to expect a harvest, is important to farmers. The calendar also may have been important in planning ceremonies to mark the seasons for planting and harvesting. It's possible that the thousands of standing stones could represent shafts of grain in a sacred field that was seen as a place of worship.

The fields of stone also may have served as ceremonial pathways for the dead. There are many large stone tombs in the area that could be related to the alignments in the fields.

The reasons for the long lines of standing stones at Carnac may never be clearly understood. We can only imagine how the patterns of stones may have helped people in Stone Age farming communities to understand the mysteries of the universe.

No one knows why thousands of carved stones were lined up on this field in France.

Etruscan Tombs

The airplane that flew over central Italy in 1944 was photographing the landscape below in an attempt to find out where the enemy had hidden their weapons. While this information was important in planning military campaigns in World War II, it also became valuable to archaeologists searching for Etruscan tombs.

Aerial photographs taken during World War II show that grass growing over a buried Etruscan tomb appears as a light circular patch. Grass growing over the stone roof of a tomb is not as dark as grass that has deeper roots. By studying the pattern of light and dark in landscape photos, archaeologists have been able to identify the underground locations of tombs.

The Etruscan people settled in central Italy 3,000 years ago. Today their cities, temples, and tombs lie in ruin. Archaeologists interested in learning more about these people have searched for their cemeteries, because Etruscan burials often contain household goods that people used in everyday life.

Specialized techniques and instruments have been developed to help in the search for buried Etruscan cemeteries. Archaeologists must first find the location of the landscape identified in the aerial photographs. The next part of the search involves sending an electrical current through the ground. An electrical current passing through the earth will move more slowly than it will passing through an empty space. By recording places where an electrical current peaks upon reaching an open space, underground tombs may be located. Once a tomb has been located, the next step is to drill a hole through the stone roof and insert a periscope camera. This camera, attached to a long tube, is used to photograph the contents and condition of the tomb before it is excavated.

When the tombs are excavated, they are often found to look like the houses that people occupied during their lifetimes. Some of the tombs were built of stone blocks, and others were carved out of solid rock. Walls were often painted with scenes of daily life, with people shown dancing, dining, or playing musical instruments. Wall paintings also show people participating in religious rituals. Painted pottery and bronze sculptures were placed in the burial chambers, along with tools and weapons.

By finding Etruscan tombs with their contents in place, archaeologists have begun to learn about the lives of this pre-Roman people.

Little is known about the Etruscans, but their tombs tell us something about their lives.

Easter Island

A speck of land in the vast reaches of the Pacific Ocean became known as Easter Island when the captain of a Dutch ship anchored there on Easter Sunday in the year 1722. When the sailors stepped ashore, they marveled at the huge stone statues looking down upon them. How could statues 20 feet tall, and weighing as much as 80 tons, be carved, transported, and set in place on platforms of stones?

In an attempt to explain how the statues were carved, a twentieth-century explorer, Thor Heyerdahl, studied the tools left behind by the original stonemasons. Hard stone chisels were used to chip away the softer volcanic rock of which the statues were made. From the unfinished works still lying in the rock quarries, it was obvious that all the carving was done while the stone was in the ground. When the front of a statue was finished, the back remained attached to the rock from which it was carved. Each stone figure was then freed by cutting it away from the rock and moving it to where it would be set in place.

Heyerdahl organized a group of workers to move one of the large statues, using the same methods as those who had put the original statues in place. The sculptures were placed on wooden logs and pulled with ropes to the platforms where they would stand.

To raise the figures, long wooden poles were used to pry up one side while small stones were placed under the statue. This was done repeatedly until the pile of stones under the statue had raised it to a point where ropes could be used to pull it to a standing position.

After the statues were raised upright, eyes of shells and coral were added to each face.

The statues served as guardians for the dead, whose bodies were placed on funerary platforms below them. When the bones had been picked clean by the birds, the bones were gathered up and placed in chambers in the funerary platforms. Families often competed with one another to see who could set up the tallest statues or biggest platforms.

The history of Easter Island is filled with scenes of violence. In tribal wars among the people, many of the statues were knocked over or broken. Stone quarries were abandoned, and statues were left unfinished or scattered in the fields.

Today, some of these giant figures have been restored to their ancient platforms. Their long, silent faces and coral eyes now gaze down upon the remaining evidence of a civilization that once flourished on this tiny, isolated island in the Pacific Ocean.

Dutch explorers were mystified when they encountered these massive stone monuments.

The Nazca Lines

A hummingbird, a monkey, a spider, a whale, and a series of straight lines—these are some of the shapes that can be seen on the desert floor of the Plain of Nazca in Peru. The meaning of these giant figures and lines is one of the great mysteries of archaeology.

The lines and figures were made by the Nazca people who lived in the coastal deserts of Peru more than 1,000 years ago. The shapes drawn on the floor of the desert are so large that they can only be recognized from the air. The lines were made by brushing aside small dark stones that covered the desert floor to expose the lighter soil beneath.

The Nazca Lines seem to crisscross in every direction. Many of them are long, and all are straight. There have been many theories to explain them. One writer claimed that they were landing fields for spacecraft from another galaxy, but scientists quickly rejected this theory. Scientific observations have shown that a number of the lines could have been used as sighting points for stars and planets. Many of the lines, however, seem to have no reference to astronomy.

A more recent theory is that the lines represent sacred pathways to religious shrines. Some Indian peoples in the region follow certain paths called "ceques" that lead them to places of worship.

The giant animal figures that also decorate the desert floor at Nazca are even more of a mystery than the lines. Some of these animal figures are half the size of a football field. The animals shown in these desert designs may have been part of a type of calendar. In ancient times, certain animals represented seasons of the year. Walking around inside a pathway that marks the shape of a certain animal may have been part of a ceremony to welcome a season. No one can be certain what the lines and figures really mean.

The desert where the Nazca Lines are located has changed very little for centuries. Rain almost never falls there. But although there has been very little erosion from natural causes, great damage has been caused by people who drive vehicles over the lines and figures. A strong effort by the Peruvian government has succeeded in stopping some of the vandalism. If the Nazca Lines are preserved, we will have a better chance to discover their meaning.

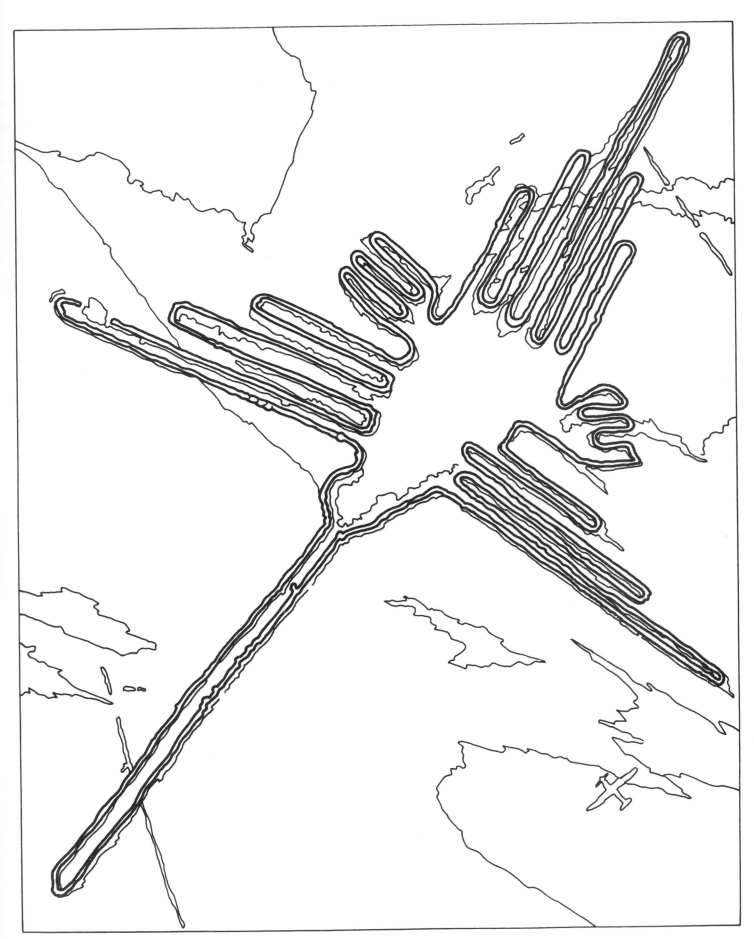

Pictured at lower right is the shadow of an airplane—tiny compared to the Nazca Lines.

Stonehenge

White-robed figures make their way across Salisbury Plain toward the circle of standing stones known as Stonehenge. This is a twentieth-century gathering of people who call themselves followers of the ancient priesthood of Druids. Each year they meet at Stonehenge, where they practice the rituals of Druids who lived in this part of England 1,500 years ago.

Some people believe that the Druids built Stonehenge as a great religious shrine. Archaeologists who have excavated Stonehenge say that the site has nothing to do with Druids. Construction at Stonehenge began 2,000 years before the Druid priesthood was established.

People have imagined many things about Stonehenge. It has been said that Stonehenge was built by the Romans as a temple to their sky god. It has also been suggested that Merlin the magician brought the great stones from Ireland by using his magical powers. Stonehenge has been seen as a place where all of the electrical and magnetic forces of the earth come together in a gigantic energy field.

Archaeologists and other scientists find no evidence to support any of these wild ideas about Stonehenge. The many scientific measurements of the monument indicate that the builders of Stonehenge had a good understanding of astronomy.

Stonehenge was built over a 1,000-year period that began around 2500 B.C. By 1500 B.C., the builders of Stonehenge had increased their knowledge of astronomy to the point where the position of each stone could more accurately record the sun, the moon, and the stars.

Stonehenge may have served as a giant computer for people in the prehistoric world. The arrangement of stones made it possible to measure the longest and shortest days of the year. It was also possible to predict eclipses from the arrangement of the stones. The phases of the moon could be calculated from the stone patterns set up inside the outer ring of stones. The seasons of the year could be identified so that farmers would know the best time to plant their crops. It was also important to know the times of the year when the seas would be calm enough for trading ships to carry on commerce.

Stonehenge is a modern marvel of prehistoric engineering and astronomy. Scientific studies of this amazing monument tell us that people living in prehistoric times used their intelligence to improve their lives.

Is Stonehenge an ancient temple? A prehistoric computer? Or both?

The Citadel at Mycenae

One of the great fortresses of the ancient world is the Citadel of Mycenae. This fortress city was built more than 3,000 years ago in what is now Greece. Some of the stones used to build the fortress weigh many tons, and legends say that the stones were set in place by a one-eyed giant called a Cyclops.

We now know that the stones were moved by a people we call the Mycenaeans. These people were skilled in the art of moving large stones to build walls, houses, palaces, and tombs.

The Mycenaeans built their fortress on a hilltop, where they had a good view of the countryside and of several mountain passes leading to the sea. This location helped them defend themselves from attack by other tribes in the region.

The main entrance to the Citadel was sealed by a large wooden door. Upon reaching this door, enemy forces would find themselves trapped between the walls leading to the door. Mycenaean warriors standing on the walls of the fortress above them could throw their spears down on their attackers from three different positions.

The archaeologist who excavated the Citadel of Mycenae, Heinrich Schliemann, found a number of grave sites where Mycenaean warriors had been buried with gold death masks. These death masks, now in the Athens Museum, bring us face to face with the warriors who defended the Citadel of Mycenae more than 3,000 years ago.

How to Build a Fortress

Using a long stick as a lever, workers could pry up one end of a large stone and hold it in place until smaller stones could be put under it. By raising the other end of the stone in the same way, they could lift the big stone onto a wooden sled. When the stone was tied to the sled, it could be moved to where it would be set in place.

By piling up dirt to form a ramp, workers could pull wooden sleds carrying the stones to higher parts of the wall.

In this way, stone by stone, a mighty fortress could be built.

From their fortified lookout, Mycenaean warriors kept their city safe—for a while.

The Lost Continent of Atlantis?

Nearly 2,500 years ago, the Greek philosopher Plato told a story about a lost civilization that had created art, music, and many beautiful buildings. Many years before Plato's time, this civilization was destroyed by earthquakes, fire, and floods, and sank into the sea. Plato called this civilization the Lost Continent of Atlantis. Recently, archaeologists digging on the Island of Crete announced that they may have found the place that Plato described.

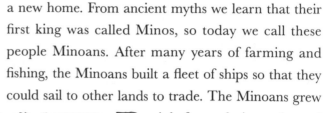

This much we know: More than 4,000 years ago, people from Asia and North Africa sailed to the Island of Crete in the Mediterranean Sea in search of a new home. From ancient myths we learn that their first king was called Minos, so today we call these people Minoans. After many years of farming and fishing, the Minoans built a fleet of ships so that they could sail to other lands to trade. The Minoans grew rich from their trade and soon began to build palaces for their royal families.

The Palace of Knossos is one of the most important buildings of the Minoan civilization. This large building had many rooms decorated with paintings of plants and flowers as well as fish and animals that lived in the sea. The royal family lived in rooms connected to bathrooms that had bathtubs and private toilets. Other rooms were used to store grain and olive oil. Like many of the palaces on Crete, Knossos had a central courtyard where religious ceremonies took place.

Bull-leaping was one event held in the courtyard. Here young boys and girls would grab a charging bull by the horns and somersault over the animal. Spectators stood on the balconies above the courtyard to watch this event, as well as dances and parades to celebrate the grain harvest.

As archaeologists continue to uncover more of the mysteries of the Minoans, they may soon be able to say with certainty whether the Minoan civilization was actually the one that gave rise to Plato's account of the Lost Continent of Atlantis.

Wall paintings decorate palaces on the island of Crete. Is this Plato's Lost Continent?

The Island of Thera

The volcano's explosion covered the sea with ash and set off a tidal wave 300 feet high. On this day nearly 3,500 years ago, an ancient civilization was destroyed.

A people we call the Minoans had established themselves on the island of Crete in the eastern Mediterranean Sea about 4,000 years ago. The Minoans soon began to establish colonies on the islands near

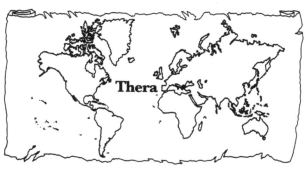

their home base in Crete. One of their colonies was located on an island called Thera, about 70 miles north of Crete. The Minoan colony on Thera settled at the base of a mile-high volcano.

The Minoans built many houses on Thera and decorated them with paintings. These paintings show us a picture of Minoan life as it was nearly 3,500 years ago. People are seen in their houses, rowing boats at sea, and playing games. In one scene, two young boys are boxing—and wearing boxing gloves. In another painting, a fisherman is carrying a fish he has caught. These pictures still exist because they were protected by being buried under ash from the great explosion of the volcano on Thera around 1500 B.C.

People living on the slopes of the volcano were going about their daily tasks when the earth began to shake. Earthquakes were common, and people paid no attention to tremors. But when smoke and ash began to erupt from the volcano, the inhabitants of Thera knew it was time to leave their island.

Soon the volcano erupted, throwing out tons of ash that buried houses and spread over the sea to nearby islands. The eruption emptied the interior of the volcanic cone, causing it to collapse. This produced an enormous explosion and a tidal wave. When the huge wall of water reached the coast of Crete, it sank hundreds of Minoan trading ships. Ports on the north shore of Crete were covered with a blanket of ash. The Minoan civilization never recovered.

Recent excavations of the Island of Thera have revealed crushed stairways, pottery that was hurled from storerooms, and buildings buried under tons of ash. The fact that few personal goods have been found suggests people must have had time to pack their things and leave the island before the major explosion.

When the volcano began to smoke, the people of Thera had to decide whether to flee.

Abu Simbel

He was a pharaoh determined to be remembered. His statue was built in every part of Egypt, and his architectural monuments were of enormous size. Rameses II became pharaoh of Egypt in 1292 B.C., and soon afterward he began an extensive building program. Of the many works ordered by Rameses II, Abu Simbel stands out.

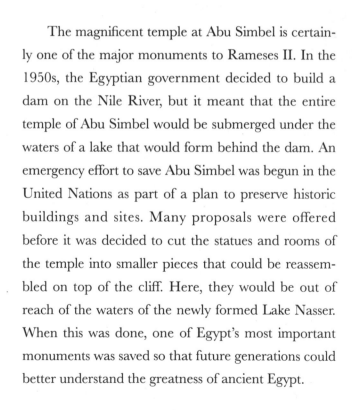

In the far reaches of Egypt, at a site called Abu Simbel along the Nile River, the stone workers of Rameses II carved four giant figures of the pharaoh out of the side of a high cliff wall. The figures were positioned to face the rising sun each morning. Each of these four gigantic stone sculptures of Rameses II was 68 feet high and weighed more than 1,000 tons. Each statue was so large that several people could stand on one of its toenails. Rameses II was not about to let anyone forget his importance as pharaoh of Egypt.

Behind the four sculptures of Rameses, stone workers cut into the cliff wall to carve out spaces as well as a passageway 200 feet long. The corridor of the passageway ends in a room where another statue of Rameses II sits with the figures of three different gods. On February 23 and October 23, the sunrise sends a beam of light down the central passageway that lights the figures of Rameses II and the gods.

The rooms at Abu Simbel that were cut out of the solid rock were decorated with paintings and carvings of Rameses II. The great battle of Rameses II against his country's enemy, the Hittites, is shown on the inner walls of the temple. One scene shows the pharaoh driving his chariot with his pet lion running at his side.

The magnificent temple at Abu Simbel is certainly one of the major monuments to Rameses II. In the 1950s, the Egyptian government decided to build a dam on the Nile River, but it meant that the entire temple of Abu Simbel would be submerged under the waters of a lake that would form behind the dam. An emergency effort to save Abu Simbel was begun in the United Nations as part of a plan to preserve historic buildings and sites. Many proposals were offered before it was decided to cut the statues and rooms of the temple into smaller pieces that could be reassembled on top of the cliff. Here, they would be out of reach of the waters of the newly formed Lake Nasser. When this was done, one of Egypt's most important monuments was saved so that future generations could better understand the greatness of ancient Egypt.

Each of these statues is so large that a person can stand on one of its toenails.

The Pyramids of Egypt

There are many questions about how the ancient Egyptians were able to build massive pyramids of stone more than 4,000 years ago. The largest of the pyramids appears to have been designed as a tomb for the Pharaoh Cheops, and it is considered to be one of the seven wonders of the ancient world. The Pyramid of Cheops is made up of more than two million blocks of stone—each weighing, on the average, two and a half tons. Many people have tried to imagine how such large stones could be moved.

Some people believe that ancient astronauts visited the earth and used their atomic-powered machines to help the Egyptians build the pyramids. Others say that liquids were poured into molds and then hardened into the stone blocks we see today. Archaeologists, who think these ideas are nonsense, have begun to find some real answers to the question of how the pyramids of Egypt were built.

The Nile River that flows through Egypt passes very close to the place where the pyramids were built. When the Nile flooded its banks, as it did every year, stones cut from nearby quarries could be floated on rafts right up to the pyramid building site.

Before any of the stones could be put in place, the ground on which the pyramid was to be built had to be perfectly flat. To level the ground, the desert sand was cleared away down to the rock surface and filled with water. Then all the rock above the water line was cut down to the level of the water, leaving the rock floor perfectly flat. Onto this level surface, stones could then be stacked to form a pyramid.

To move the huge stones, the Egyptians placed them on wooden sleds and pulled them up a sand ramp to where they could be set in place. As the pyramid rose, the sand ramps were wrapped around the building to form a path along which the stones could be pulled. When the stones reached the spot where they were to be set, workers used levers to lift the stones from the sled and slide them into place.

When the stonework of the pyramid was completed, the sand ramps were removed and the entire structure was covered with slabs of polished stone. Some of this outer cover may still be seen today.

To better understand how the pyramids were built, archaeologists constructed a small pyramid using the tools and methods of the ancient Egyptians. The results of their experiment proved that the people who built the great pyramids of Egypt were able to do so without the help of ancient astronauts or magic formulas for liquid stone.

Stone by stone, the pyramids were built with the help of levers, sleds, and ropes.

The Ships of the Pharaoh

Forty-six centuries had passed since the Egyptian Pharaoh Cheops had been buried with great ceremony in the pyramid that bears his name. In recent years, the south side of his pyramid had become a dumping ground for rocks and sand that had been dug out in earlier excavations. The year was 1954, and the time had come to clear away the material that had gathered at the base of the Pyramid of Cheops.

As workmen removed the pile of sand and rock, a wall suddenly appeared and a cut stone floor at the base of the wall came into view. The wall was recognized as a boundary around the Great Pyramid of Cheops to set it apart from other buildings. The mystery of this next section of the wall was that it stood closer to the pyramid than other known sections of the same wall. Had this been built to hide something underneath it? The archaeologist who decided to answer this question made a spectacular discovery.

When workmen dug deeper at the base of the wall, they came upon several large limestone blocks. Removing the sand around the blocks, they found a ledge on which the blocks rested. As the digging continued, 41 of these blocks were revealed. Further along the side of the pyramid, a similar row of 40 large limestone blocks were found. Archaeologists soon realized that these stones covered two deep pits that had been sealed when the Pharaoh was buried.

Egyptian pharaohs were often buried with funerary boats, in imitation of the boat their sun god used to sail across the heavens. Certain that the newly uncovered limestone blocks concealed the funerary boats of the pharaoh, the archaeologists cut a small hole in one of the limestone blocks to have a look. When a mirror was used to flash a beam of sunlight into the darkness, the spotlight fell on the timbers of an ancient ship.

The boat in the pit was found in a number of sections that had been carefully stacked in layers. More than a thousand pieces were removed and assembled to rebuild the royal ship of the pharaoh. This magnificent vessel, half the length of a football field, may now be seen in a museum that has been built over the excavated boat pit. Another royal ship that lies buried in the second boat pit will remain unexcavated, to preserve it for a future time.

The Egyptians believed that their sun god sailed the heavens in a boat like this.

Tutankhamen's Tomb

He became pharaoh of Egypt at the age of nine. At the age of eighteen, the young king Tutankhamen was buried in the Valley of the Kings, a hilly desert-like area near the Egyptian city of Luxor.

Many other pharaohs were buried here in tombs that were cut into the solid rock of the hillsides. By the twentieth century, all of the tombs in this valley had been looted or destroyed, except for that of the

Pharaoh Tutankhamen. His was the only tomb that had not been found.

The discoverer of the tomb of Tutankhamen was a British archaeologist named Howard Carter. He had been digging in the Valley of the Kings for six years before he made a sensational discovery on November 4, 1922. Carter later wrote that the day of the discovery was "the day of days, the most wonderful that I have ever lived through, whose like I could never hope to see again."

What happened on the morning of the great find may have been the result of a child playing in the sand while his father, a member of the excavation team, worked nearby. It seems that the child was brushing the sand when a cut block of stone appeared. When the workmen noticed this, they cleared away more of the sand to reveal a single step. Digging further, a flight of 16 steps leading to a

sealed door appeared. Carter arrived in time to see the stairway being cleared. The stairway was quickly buried to protect the site and to give Carter enough time to get equipment to explore this new find.

When Carter returned to the Valley of the Kings three weeks later, the stairway was cleared again, and the first sealed door to the tomb was opened.

A corridor behind the door had been filled with crushed stones. These had to be removed to reach a second sealed door. Carter cut an opening into the second door and looked into the first room of the tomb chamber.

Asked, "Can you see anything?" Carter replied, "Yes, wonderful things." He was looking at a room filled with gold—a golden throne, gilded couches, statues decorated with gold, and several chariots, all glistening with gold.

It took ten years to empty the tomb and catalog all the thousands of things that were found.

King Tut's tomb is one of the most significant archaeological discoveries in history. Today, the enormous treasure of King Tutankhamen is displayed in the museum of the city of Cairo, where the world can gaze upon the splendors of an Egyptian pharaoh's tomb.

When he stepped inside Tut's tomb, Howard Carter found a room filled with gold.

The Mask of King Tut

When Howard Carter stepped into the tomb of King Tut in 1922, he was the first person to enter the burial chamber in more than 3,000 years.

Of the four chambers that formed the tomb, the burial chamber held the most spectacular find. Inside the burial chamber was a large sarcophagus. As Carter's team carefully looked inside, they found a coffin—and within it was another coffin, decorated with gold.

When they lifted the lid of the second coffin, they found a third coffin. This coffin was a life-sized mummy case more than six feet long—and it was made of solid gold. It contained the mummy of the King Tutankhamen, and over the head and shoulders of the mummy was a mask of solid gold.

The golden mask gave archaeologists a glimpse of what the king had looked like—a handsome young man with somewhat narrow eyes and full lips. On the forehead of the mask are a serpent and a vulture, and these are thought to be symbols of the two kingdoms that King Tut ruled over, Upper Egypt and Lower Egypt.

Carter's team found treasures of incredible value in King Tut's tomb. The tomb was furnished with hundreds of precious objects and even furniture, including three beds, two chairs, many statues, chairs, and footstools, as well as food and precious oils. Yet the young king was one of the least important of the 30 or so pharaohs buried in the Valley of the Kings.

The Valley of the Kings is located in a dry region, but the area sometimes has heavy rains and flash floods. It's possible that a flash flood caused a landslide that covered the entrance to King Tut's tomb with a thick layer of mud and rock that hid it from grave robbers for 3,000 years.

This teenage king ruled for only a few years before he died of unknown causes.

The Emperor's Army

Hoping to find water, a farmer in China began to dig a well. What he found was beyond imagining—an army of 7,000 life-size soldiers that had been standing guard at a hidden tomb for 2,000 years.

The soldiers were the guards of the royal tomb of China's first emperor, Shih-Huang-Ti, who became emperor of China in the year 221 B.C. He unified his country by building roads, canals, and by making sure that everyone in China used the same standard for weights and measures.

To many people, the emperor was considered to be a cruel tyrant. He put to death anyone who disagreed with him. He exiled people to faraway places where they were forced to build a great wall around China. Many thousands of workers died of cold, hunger, and hard labor while building this wall. There were many unsuccessful plots to kill the emperor. Once the emperor was told that he would die if he slept in the same room twice, so he ordered many palaces to be built, some with more than a thousand rooms—and each night he slept in a different room.

Before the emperor died, he made elaborate plans for his burial. Orders were given to create a 7,000-man army to protect his tomb. Life-size clay soldiers in full battle armor were made in the royal workshops. Soldiers, charioteers with horses, crossbow men, and carriages were produced to guard the royal burial site.

Attention was paid to every detail in the warrior figures. The faces of the soldiers are different from one another. Many figures look like portraits of warriors that may have served the emperor during his lifetime. The armor worn by the soldiers is also made of clay, but it looks like the armor worn by live soldiers. Figures of archers even have treads on the bottom of their shoes, as if to give them better footing when they shoot their crossbows.

Archaeologists have excavated many of the rooms where the emperor's army stood guard. Now the tomb of the emperor himself may soon be excavated. The mysteries it will reveal are eagerly awaited throughout the world.

These clay soldiers have stood guard at a Chinese emperor's tomb for 2,000 years.

The Great Wall of China

It has been called the eighth wonder of the world, and one of the greatest human constructions on earth. Some claim that it is big enough to be seen from the moon. The Great Wall of China winds like a giant dragon over the mountains, valleys, and deserts of China's most distant northern borders.

The Great Wall was built as a complex defense system with more than 1,000 fortified passes, 10,000 beacon towers, and a vast number of fortresses. At one time, more than a million soldiers were stationed as guards at the Great Wall. Its beacon towers flashed fire signals to one another at night and smoke signals during the day. This form of communication was necessary for a line of defense that stretched more than 1,000 miles.

Towns grew up in areas near the wall to support soldiers and their families in this remote region of China. To some people, however, the Great Wall was not just a system of defense, but a line separating the high civilization of China from the barbarians beyond the wall.

No one will ever be able to count the thousands upon thousands of persons who died of disease, starvation, and brutality while building the wall. Workers froze to death in the winter and died in the scorching heat of the summer. Forced labor at the wall was punishment for people who committed crimes or offended the emperor. Many of those who died were buried in the wall and forgotten. Those who remained alive had to deal with blinding dust, howling winds, and the backbreaking labor of carrying heavy stones up steep mountain slopes. Loneliness and isolation produced many sad songs and poems that tell of the pain that workers felt as they struggled to build the wall.

There is no doubt that the Great Wall is an outstanding architectural achievement. To some it will live only as a memory of slave labor and war. China has now begun to collect money to restore the wall as a symbol of the spirit of the Chinese people.

The longest wall in the world was built to protect the boundaries of China.

Tombs of the Ming Dynasty

A giant stone tortoise marks the beginning of a journey to the royal tombs of China in the fifteenth and sixteenth centuries. A stone slab on the turtle's back is inscribed with words of tribute for the rulers of the Ming Dynasty. Housed in a fine pavilion, it stands at the beginning of the royal Spirit Path. The coffin of the emperor of China was carried along this path on the way to its final resting place.

At the start of the Spirit Path, two stone columns serve as guideposts for the soul of the emperor. Thirty-six statues of animals, warriors, and court officials, lined up in pairs, stand along both sides of the Spirit Path. All these figures are there to bring good fortune to the emperor. Most of the animal sculptures represent real animals, but two are mythical beasts. In each pair of animals, one stands while the other sits—perhaps to show that one is standing guard while the other rests. At the end of the Spirit Path stand four soldiers, four court officials, and four ministers of state.

The Spirit Path leads to the burial grounds of the Ming Dynasty are located. The burial chambers, made of stone blocks, were covered with mounds of earth made to look like the natural landscape.

The selection of a burial site depended on the findings of geomancers, people in charge of locating places where spirit forces in the earth would bring good luck. The geomancers were careful to avoid sites where they found evil spirits.

The burial chambers of the Ming Dynasty emperors varied in size and importance. Some rulers took great care in preparing their tombs, while others, possibly because they were occupied by matters of war or famine, gave little attention to their burial places.

Several tombs are large underground chambers with high arched ceilings. Porcelain pots filled with oil were placed within these burial chambers as eternal lights. When they exhausted the supply of oxygen in the tombs, they were extinguished.

Treasures of gold, jade, ivory, and silk were common in royal burials. Furniture and ceremonial objects also were placed in the tombs. To prevent thieves from entering, the doors were locked, but even so, many of these tombs have been broken into and vandalized.

Archaeologists are still at work excavating and restoring the Ming tombs.

Lifelike statues line the Spirit Path, the road to the tombs of the Ming rulers.

The Plaster Figures of Pompeii

Bread had just been put into the ovens when the ground began to shake and an explosion sent great clouds of fire and ash over the city of Pompeii. The eruption of the volcano Vesuvius in 79 A.D. filled the streets of the city with ash up to the second floor of the houses. People fled their homes by climbing out of second-story windows. Some took roof tiles from the buildings to hold over their heads as protection from falling debris. Others took pillows to protect their children as they fled.

Electricity in the air triggered a sudden rainstorm that turned the dust-filled air into mud. People running to escape the explosions of Vesuvius suddenly found themselves being buried by a rain of mud. Many people suffocated from the gases in the air, and their bodies were covered by mud.

In this century, archaeologists have found hollow cavities in places where people fell and were covered by the rain of mud. The bodies of these individuals left clear impressions in the mud that could be recovered using new excavation techniques.

First, a hole was made in the hardened mud mound that had formed around the body. Gases that form when a body disintegrates are dangerous, and had to be drawn out of the mound. After this was done, liquid plaster was poured into the cavity of the mound. This filled all of the spaces that had originally been taken up by the buried body. When the plaster hardened, the mound was removed to expose the plaster cast.

What usually emerged was a plaster cast that looked like the body of the person who had died nearly 2,000 years ago. Some of these plaster casts capture the expressions of the individuals at the moment of their deaths. Some casts show women holding babies in their arms, and others show people clinging to their pet dogs.

The plaster recovery technique used at Pompeii records a moment in time when people suffered a tragic fate. We have now come to know something about these people 2,000 years later. The plaster has picked up the patterns of the fibers in their clothing and the shapes of the flowers that grew in their gardens. Excavations have shown us their houses, their theaters, their stadium, and the burnt remains of bread in their bake ovens. The plaster molds, however, have shown us the faces of the people who lived and died in the shadow of Vesuvius.

These plaster casts are memorials to men and women who were buried by a volcanic eruption.

Machu Picchu

High in the Andes of Peru is the hidden site of an ancient Inca city. The great civilization of the Incas that once stretched along the west coast of South America was centered in the mountain ranges of Peru. One of the many outposts of that civilization was the fortress city called Machu Picchu.

The city of Machu Picchu was hidden in its high mountain location for many years until it was discovered by the explorer Hiram Bingham in 1911. Bingham had great difficulty reaching the mountaintop, and the ruins of the city had become covered with jungle growth. When the trees and vines were cut away, Bingham was surprised to see buildings made of perfectly cut and fitted stones. The Inca craftsmen had learned to work large stones of great

hardness with skill and patience. Their stonework is considered to be one of the marvels of ancient civilizations.

The buildings of Machu Picchu seem to wrap around a high rock formation that stands between two mountain peaks. Agricultural terraces hang on the mountainside like giant stairways. Stones projecting from the walls of buildings serve as ladders to higher levels of the city. Long flights of stairs connecting parts of the city to one another were controlled by large gateways that could be closed to prevent an enemy invasion.

A strangely cut stone altar, known as the hitching post of the sun, still stands on a high point overlooking the city of Machu Picchu. Here Inca priests performed a ceremony to represent tying the sun to a stone shaft that projected from the altar. This was done on the shortest day of the year. Seeing the sun become lower and lower on the horizon as the shortest day approached, people felt that the sun would eventually disappear. It was believed that the ceremony of tethering the sun to the "hitching post" would prevent the sun from disappearing.

The mountainside setting of Machu Picchu was an inspiration to a great civilization that worshiped the sun.

Once a mighty city was built in the Andes Mountains of Peru—then it was abandoned.

Sacsahuaman

No one could believe that the fortress protecting the ancient Inca city of Cuzco in Peru was made by human hands. Some of the stones in this structure weigh 200 tons, and several are more than 20 feet high. How these stones were hauled from distant quarries is still a mystery. As many as 20,000 people worked for more than half a century to build this giant stone fortress more than 500 years ago.

The fortified stone walls of Sacsahuaman rise on three earthen terraces. A zigzag pattern of stone walls runs along the length of each terrace. The walls, more than 50 feet high, present a major obstacle to anyone attacking the fortress. An invader would have to climb three sets of zigzag walls to reach the top of the hill that overlooks the Inca city of Cuzco. A strange thing about this fortress is that the Inca had no enemy strong enough to attack their capital city.

The Inca produced some of the finest stone work ever crafted by human hands. By grinding the surfaces of the stone perfectly flat, they could fit the stones together without the use of mortar. Walls were held together by the weight of the stones on top of one another.

Stones were often notched together to keep them from sliding apart. The walls of Sacsahuaman are locked together in an elaborate pattern of notched stone. Some of the notched stones lock into as many as eight other stones in the wall. This method of construction gave the stone walls great strength. Inca stonework fits together so perfectly that a knife blade cannot be inserted between the stones.

Sacsahuaman is in a region where earthquakes are common. Inca builders produced structures that can withstand severe earthquakes. The Europeans who conquered the Inca empire placed their buildings on top of Inca walls. Earthquakes shattered these buildings, but left the Inca walls unharmed.

Architects in the twentieth century have studied Inca methods of stone construction to learn how modern buildings might best be built in earthquake zones. The genius of the Inca builders tells us that we have much to learn from the past.

Leading his llamas past an ancient Inca fortress at Cuzco is a present-day farmer.

Copan

Once there was a busy Maya city in Central America, a city with a rich culture. Then, jungle growth and the waters of the Copan River claimed the ancient Maya city of Copan in Honduras.

More than a century ago, John Lloyd Stephens and Frederic Catherwood explored this great ceremonial center of the Maya civilization. They found the magnificent monuments of this once-proud city tangled in vines and vegetation.

The Maya carved tall shafts of stone that we call stele. These were done to commemorate special events and important people. The stele of Copan represent a variety of priests, warriors, and kings. Each figure is shown in an elaborate costume with an ornate headdress. In each figure beads, jewelry, feather work, clothing, sandals, masks, and scepters are carved in fine detail. Maya ceremonies must have been an impressive display of costumes in a setting of magnificent architecture.

Pyramids, ball courts, temples, and altars surround the plaza where many of the carved stele now stand. Shadows created by the late afternoon sun emphasize the sculptural details of the stone carvings. The faces of the figures represented in the stele have the same features that we see in the faces of the Maya people today. In a number of stele, figures wear a headdress that holds the mask of a deity. Altars at the bases of the stele may have been meant for offerings to the gods represented by the masks.

The sides and backs of the stele often display glyph writing. Glyphs are carved figures or shapes that represent words or names in the ancient Maya language.

The stele of Copan give us a clear picture of the Maya kings and the astronomer priests who lived here 1,500 years ago. At Copan there is a broad stairway, covered with hundreds of glyphs, that leads to the top of a pyramid. After this stairway is restored and its glyphs translated, we may learn more about the people portrayed in the stele.

Reading the Stones

The Mayan language had long remained a mystery until recent discoveries unlocked some of its secrets. Archaeologists can now read some of its inscriptions and dates.

A number system was part of the glyph writing. The Maya wrote their numbers using a circle or dot as the number one, and a bar as the number five. In this system the number eight is a bar with three dots and the number ten is two bars.

Numbers on the stele seem to refer to the age of the kings who were represented by the stone carvings.

The language of the Maya people is carved in stone, but much of it is still a mystery.

Tikal

Screaming monkeys running across the treetops, thick vines hanging from the dense jungle canopy, the strange sounds of birds, and armies of leafcutter ants marching along the jungle floor provide the setting for the ancient Maya city of Tikal in Guatemala. Here giant causeways crisscross the uneven surface of the landscape. Plazas and court-yards open into unexpected spaces. Large slabs of carved stone stand like silent sen-tinels amid moss-covered temples, altars, and shrines.

The pyramids of Tikal are very tall, with steep stairs and a temple at the top. Maya priests climbing the stairs must have seemed to be walking up to the heavens. Inside the temples, priests performed cere-monies that were often related to the sun, moon, and stars. The high pyramids made it possible to get above the tall jungle trees to watch the heavens. Maya beliefs were based on the sa-cred calendar developed by observing the movements of the planets.

Tikal was one of many cities built by the ancient Maya in the midst of a jungle. To live in this dense jungle, the Maya constructed reservoirs to hold rain-water. Fruits and seeds from a wide variety of plants had to be gathered and stored. While some animals could be hunted for food, others presented great danger. Poisonous snakes, deadly insects, and fierce ants made life difficult and risky.

Even though jungle life presented many hard-ships, the Maya people constructed magnificent buildings, large ceremonial plazas, and high pyramids.

The Maya placed a number of large stone slabs in front of their pyramids. These stone monuments, called stele, were usually put in place to mark a specific event. They often refer to a ruler who has come to power or an event in astronomy. Many of these stele are covered with writing in the form of figures called glyphs.

Scientists are working very hard to unlock the se-crets of Maya glyph writing. They hope to learn more about the people who built large cities and trading centers in the thick jungle of Central America.

The city of Tikal was abandoned about 1,000 years ago and covered by the jungle.

The Pyramids of Mexico

It was a strange sight to see a reed boat being built in the shadows of the great pyramids of Egypt. A twentieth-century explorer, Thor Heyerdahl, was building the boat to prove that Egyptians could have sailed from Egypt to Mexico thousands of years before Columbus. This might explain how the ancient Mexican civilization learned to build pyramids.

Did the Egyptians teach the people of ancient Mexico how to build pyramids? Most archaeologists don't think so—but let's see why.

The pyramid-building age in Egypt ended 2,000 years before pyramid-building began in ancient Mexico. It seems strange that ideas brought to Mexico would not be used for several thousand years. There are also great differences between Egyptian and Mexican pyramids. A temple usually stands on the flat top of a Mexican pyramid, while an Egyptian pyramid comes to a point. In Mexico, stairs on the outside of a pyramid lead to a temple at the top. Egyptian pyramids have inner passageways that lead to a room or burial chamber. Almost all Egyptian pyramids were built as tombs, but very few Mexican pyramids contain tombs or burials.

In Mexico it is common to find one pyramid inside another. New pyramids were often built over older pyramids. In Egypt, this was not the case. In Egypt, where there is very little rain, pyramids have smooth, sloping sides. In Mexico, which has a rainy season, pyramids have terraced sides to slow down the rush of water that could wash away the stone work and plaster that cover the pyramid.

Thor Heyerdahl successfully sailed the reed boat he had built from Egypt to the Americas. His voyage does suggest that sailors from ancient Egypt could have brought their ideas about pyramid building to the civilizations of ancient Mexico. To archaeologists, however, the differences between Mexican and Egyptian pyramids are evidence that the civilizations of ancient Mexico developed their own ideas about pyramid building from their own religion and their own environment.

To study pyramids in Mexico and Egypt, Thor Heyerdahl built a reed boat like this one.

The Tomb at Palenque

Planning to make a routine survey, Dr. Alberto Ruz entered the Temple of the Inscriptions at Palenque in Mexico. The circular shapes in the corners of the stone slabs covering the floor of the temple seemed a bit unusual to him. It looked as if they might be finger holes sealed with stone plugs. If they were finger holes, the stone slabs could be lifted up by gripping the stones through the finger holes. The stone plugs were knocked out of the holes, and the stones were lifted from the floor—revealing a stairwell that seemed to lead to a chamber below the pyramid.

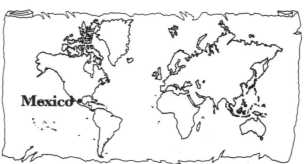

After four seasons of careful archaeological work, the stone and rubble was removed from the stairwell. The stairs that had been revealed led down into the interior of the pyramid and into a burial chamber. Here a large sarcophagus held the body and the treasures of an ancient Maya king. This discovery, on June 13, 1952, helped archaeologists understand the burial customs of Maya royalty.

Many of the royal tombs in the Maya region of Mexico and Guatemala have been destroyed by tomb robbers. It is very difficult for an archaeologist to do a proper study of a burial site if it has been looted or disturbed. The royal tomb that Dr. Ruz found in Palenque was in perfect condition, having remained sealed and undisturbed for 1,300 years.

The skeletons of five young people were found at the entrance to the burial chamber, perhaps put there to accompany the king on his journey to the next world. A huge sarcophagus covered by a carved stone lid took up much of the space in the burial chamber. The carving on the lid of the sarcophagus showed the king suspended between the heavens and the under-world. A sacred Ceiba tree, or tree of life, seemed to grow out of the king's body, while the jaws of an earth monster reached up to swallow him. This un-usual carving was a way of showing belief in what would happen to a royal person after his death.

The skull of the king revealed a jade bead in his mouth and a number of teeth that had been fitted with small pieces of jade. A jade mosaic death mask had been placed over the head of the king, and neck-laces of jade had been placed around the mask.

The many interesting burial customs of the an-cient Maya might have been lost forever if this important tomb of a Maya king had not been found.

Steep stairs lead to the stone tomb of a Maya king buried more than 1,000 years ago.

The Ball Court at Chichén Itzá

On a court enclosed by high walls, players kept a heavy rubber ball in motion. Spectators standing on top of the walls watched the action of players as they struck the ball with their heavily padded bodies. Players tried to knock the ball through a vertical stone ring set high in the center of the wall—without using their hands or feet. Getting the ball through the ring was a very difficult thing to do, and games often lasted for several days.

Ball games were very popular among civilizations of the ancient Americas. Ball courts were built in Mexico and Central America long before Columbus arrived in the New World. These courts had many different architectural styles, as well as different rules about how to play the game.

One of the most famous ball courts was located in the ancient Maya city of Chichén Itzá, in Mexico's Yucatan Peninsula. This large ball court had a long playing field set between two high walls. Sounds were magnified by the walls on either side of the court. Whispers could easily be heard from one end of the ball court to the other end. Temples stood at either end of the playing fields.

Many ceremonies and rituals were associated with the ball game. The ball may have represented the sun. Putting the ball through the stone ring may have been a way to represent the sun passing across the sky in celebration of a certain day of the year. Scenes of the ceremonies were carved into stone slabs set along the lower sections of the walls. Some of these carvings show a ball player being sacrificed to the gods. This may have been a player who succeeded in knocking the ball through the stone ring. To sacrifice his life was considered an honor, and the player was believed to live among the gods. At night the rubber ball was set up as an object of worship, and dancing and ceremonies honored the ball.

Through their ball game, the Maya people found ways to honor their gods.

Sport may have been a matter of life and death to the Maya people.

The Castle at Chichén Itzá

In the bright sunshine of March, a crowd gathers at the foot of a pyramid in Mexico's Yucatan Peninsula. It is March 21, the spring equinox, when the number of hours of daylight and nighttime are the same.

The pyramid at Chichén Itzá appears to have been built by the Maya people more than a thousand years ago as a calendar in stone. On the top of the flat pyramid stands a temple.

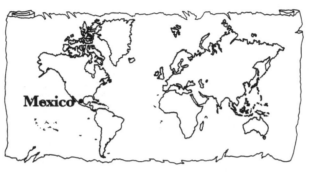

Stairways on all four sides of the pyramid lead up to the temple. Flat strips of stone on each side of the main stairway lead down to a large stone head of a snake at the bottom of the stairway. At the time of the spring equinox, sunlight falling across the terraces creates a wavy pattern of light on the edge of the stairs that ends in the head of the snake.

On the day of the spring equinox, the angle of sunlight spilling across the terraces forms a pattern that looks like a moving snake. People gathered here in ancient times on March 21 to see the snake pattern and to celebrate the event of the equinox. Even today, thousands of persons gather in the plaza every March 21 to witness this event.

When conquerors from Spain saw the pyramid at Chichén Itzá, they named it "El Castillo," because they thought that it looked like a castle. They had no way of knowing that buried inside El Castillo was another pyramid with a treasure in its temple.

Archaeologists digging inside the pyramid found a stairway leading to this temple. Upon entering the temple chamber, they saw a "Chac-Mool," a reclining carved stone figure holding a plate on his chest. The Maya people believed that Chac-Mool figures were messengers to the gods. Behind the Chac-Mool stood a fierce-looking stone jaguar that had been painted red and decorated with green jade spots. Under the jaguar was a small dish set with many precious stones.

The great pyramid of Chichén Itzá, known as El Castillo, has revealed two of its secrets: the snake pattern at the time of the equinox, and the treasure of a temple buried inside the pyramid. There are probably many more mysteries yet to be explored at El Castillo.

Inside this pyramid is another pyramid, and within is a temple once filled with treasure.

The Treasure of Tomb Seven

It was New Year's Day in 1932 when a young Mexican archaeologist, Dr. Alfonso Caso, decided to dig at tomb number seven at the site of Monte Alban in southern Mexico. After several days, Dr. Caso reached the floor of the tomb—but found only a few artifacts. The empty tomb appeared to have been looted. But as members of the excavation team walked across the floor of the tomb, they heard echoes. Could there be another room below the floor?

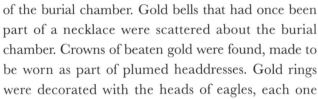
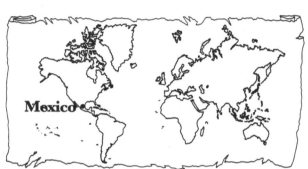

When a hole was opened to see what might be beneath the floor, a lower tomb chamber was revealed. Squeezing into the newly discovered room, Dr. Caso found himself ankle-deep in gold. He had found the burial place of an important person whose tomb had been sealed for more than 700 years.

The treasure of Tomb Seven included objects made of turquoise, pearls, silver, and gold. Gold discs of the sun and gold masks of the gods littered the floor of the burial chamber. Gold bells that had once been part of a necklace were scattered about the burial chamber. Crowns of beaten gold were found, made to be worn as part of plumed headdresses. Gold rings were decorated with the heads of eagles, each one carrying a golden sun disc in its beak. Rings bore the face of the god of spring. One golden pendant in the form of a ball court was decorated with figures that appeared to be playing the game.

Nine people had been buried in the tomb. Their skeletons revealed that they were all males, ranging in age from 16 to 60. One of the skeletons wore ten bracelets and appeared to be the most important person in the group.

The treasures of Tomb Seven, more than 500 pieces altogether, are counted among the most important archaeological discoveries of ancient Mexico.

The Lost Wax Method

Studies of Tomb Seven have revealed the unusual way in which some of the gold jewelry was made. A process called the "lost wax method" was used to make some of the gold pieces.

First, a small figure or mask would be carved in wax. The wax image would then be coated with liquid clay until a ball of clay formed around the wax figure. When the clay hardened, molten gold would be poured into an opening that reached down in the enclosed wax image. The molten gold would immediately melt the wax, turning it into steam that would escape through an opening in the clay ball. When the gold had completely replaced the wax image, the clay ball would be broken open to take out the gold—now hardened into the exact image of the wax model.

The lost wax process for casting gold shows the genius of the people who made these treasures at Monte Alban more than 700 years ago.

A golden chest ornament and mask was found among the Treasure of Tomb Seven.

The Temple Mountains of Angkor Wat

The jungle vines that wind around the temples hide a dramatic story carved in stone—scenes of war and conquest with thousands of elephants crushing the enemies of a powerful people called the Khmers. These people lived in what is now Cambodia, in Southeast Asia.

The Khmers controlled a large region known as Indochina from the 9th to the 16th century A.D. During this time, they conquered and enslaved many other peoples. Little was known about the Khmers until the middle of the 19th century, when a French explorer, Henri Mauhot, came upon the abandoned Khmer city of Angkor Wat deep in the Cambodian jungles. His writings interested many people in his discovery of a mysterious city and a lost civilization.

The jungle had overtaken Angkor Wat. As the vines and trees were cleared, a city began to appear—with fantastic temples, palaces, gateways, and plazas. Archaeologists were amazed at the size of the buildings. One temple was so large that it must have needed a quarter of a million servants. Palaces for wealthy Khmer families had as many as one hundred servants. Common household items such as dishes and spoons were made of gold, and many of the temples were decorated with gold.

The riches that supported this powerful society and its rulers came from agriculture. The great Mekong River that flowed through the Khmer region made the land fertile and provided people with fish as well as a means of transportation.

The Khmers learned to control the waters of the river by building canals and irrigation systems. They even created artificial lakes and reservoirs to supply water to crops during the dry season.

Each Khmer king built a temple to show his power and importance—and each king wanted a temple bigger and higher than those built by earlier rulers. This led to the construction of enormous buildings decorated with beautiful stone carvings of the Khmer people dancing, boating, and waging war. These temple mountains, as they were called, were designed to reach toward the sky so that rulers could join the gods in the heavens.

The magnificent architecture of temples, gateway sculpture, walls, and reflecting pools proclaimed the glory of the Khmer empire for hundreds of years, until it was all swallowed by the jungles of Southeast Asia.

Beautiful temples and stone carvings are reminders of a powerful society, long vanished.

The Sutton Hoo Ship Burial

Mrs. Edith May Pretty had no idea that a treasure ship was buried in her backyard. But in July of 1939, archaeologists excavated a 1,300-year-old ship on Mrs. Pretty's farm in England. Along with the remains of a ship, they discovered precious stones, weapons, armor, a helmet, belt buckles, drinking vessels, and gold coins.

All these items had been placed in a ship that may have contained the body of an Anglo-Saxon chieftain who was buried around 625 A.D. It was the custom of Vikings and other tribes living in northern Europe to bury their dead in funerary ships. The ships were sailed to the burial site with the body and the treasure of the person to be buried. Upon arriving at the burial site, the ship would be dragged overland to a trench where it would be buried and covered with a mound of earth.

The Sutton Hoo farm site, where the treasure ship was found, is located in England along the shores of the Deben River. In the seventh century A.D., this area was occupied by a tribe known as the Wolf People. The region contains a number of ancient burial mounds that have been looted. In the seventeenth century, robbers searching for treasure had dug into the mound where the Sutton Hoo ship was buried. The robbers had cut a tunnel into the mound and just missed finding the ship.

One of the great mysteries of the burial is that no body was found. Did the body and its bones disintegrate in the acid soil? If so, why were no rings or clothing fragments found? Scientists looked for chemicals in the soil that would indicate the presence of a human body. They did find some evidence of chemicals in the soil that would have formed where a body would have decayed. But the evidence was not enough to confirm the existence of a body. The question of what happened to the person who was to have been buried in the ship is still unanswered.

The treasures of the Sutton Hoo ship burial contain a number of objects made of gold and silver. The lid of a purse that held 37 gold coins was decorated with gold shapes of birds and wolf-like animals. Fragments of a warrior's helmet show that it had been trimmed with silver.

Mrs. Pretty donated all of the findings to the British Museum in London. Today, any visitor to the museum can see the treasure that was almost lost to the grave robbers who came within inches of finding the Sutton Hoo ship.

The Vikings built funeral ships like this one, which was discovered on an English farm.

The Alhambra Palace

The mysteries of the Alhambra Palace are reflected in its strange beauty. Located in southern Spain, in the city of Granada, the Alhambra served as a fortress for the Moorish kings from northern Africa who ruled Spain in the 13th and 14th centuries.

Many of the walls in rooms of the Alhambra Palace are covered with intricate designs and colorful patterns that delight the eyes. Most of the decoration was done with tiles that could be assembled in a variety of patterns.

It has been said that people who live in great open spaces tend to create artworks crowded with details that fill up the entire surface of the design space. From the deserts of North Africa, nomadic Moorish invaders had come into a land of snow-capped mountains and abundant waters. They had never seen such landscapes before, but they were forbidden by their religion to represent it in a realistic style. The Moslem faith that the invaders brought into Spain did not allow them to represent human, animal, or plant forms in any realistic way. So their art consists of patterns and designs that do not show images of living things. They did, however, have sayings from their sacred book, the Koran, gracefully lettered and blended into the complicated design patterns.

Plaster also was used to decorate the ceilings of the palace rooms. Plaster can be carved or molded into many different forms. Some of the plaster designs in the ceilings look like stalactites hanging from the roof of a cave. The plaster patterns were ornamented with gold.

Melting snow from the nearby Sierra Nevada Mountains provided the builders of the Alhambra Palace with water that could be used to create fountains and reflecting pools. The water adds beauty and a sense of calm to the palace. Pools of water placed in the courtyards of the building reflect the colorful designs of the tile work. Horseshoe-shaped arches supported on thin columns surround the courtyard space, and their highly decorated forms seem to float in the reflecting pools. The sound of water bubbling from the fountains adds to the peaceful atmosphere.

Fountains, reflecting pools, and complex designs in the decoration, plaster work, and courtyards were created by nomads to create a place of beauty and faith at the Alhambra Palace.

The people who built this palace were Moslems from northern Africa called Moors.

Mesa Verde

A light snow fell as two cowboys searching for stray cattle rode to the top of a Colorado mesa to get a better view of the canyon below. As they looked across the canyon, a strange sight appeared through the snowfall. It looked as if a city had been built into a cave-like opening on the side of a nearby mesa. Curious about what they saw, Richard Wetherill and Charles Mason rode their horses to a spot where the city appeared before them. It was here, in December of 1888, that they discovered one of the largest cliff dwellings of the Anasazi.

Cliff Palace, as their discovery was named, had been part of a large complex of cliff dwellings in southern Colorado that are now part of Mesa Verde National Park. The region was settled more than 1,500 years ago by a group of Indians known as the Anasazi.

Arriving in the Mesa Verde plateau sometime after 500 A.D., the Anasazi used the many natural caves in the area as their home. Later groups of Anasazi built pit houses by digging holes into the floor of the caves and covering them with wooden frames. Some groups moved out of the caves to build houses on top of the mesa. Along the flat top of the mesa, they began to farm by planting corn, beans, and squash. For reasons that are not clear, later groups began to move back into the caves, where they built towers, houses, and storerooms of mud and stone.

Mesa Verde National Park is a wonderful place to see the way the Anasazi lived long ago. Visitors may climb into caves and see houses, towers, paintings, and carvings.

Ceremonial chambers called kivas are found throughout the Mesa Verde region. These were large, circular openings dug into the earth and covered with a roof of logs, sticks, and mud. Kivas were sacred places where the spirit world could be worshiped. Many present-day Indian peoples in the southwest United States worship in kivas. Archaeologists study these present-day Indian peoples to better understand the customs of ancient Indian societies.

Pictures in Stone

The Anasazi people painted and carved many figures and signs on the stone walls of their homes.

These painted figures are called pictographs, and those that are carved are called petroglyphs.

These symbols have been studied for more than a hundred years, but archaeologists are still puzzled by their meanings.

Just by accident, American cowboys discovered the lost city of the Anasazi people.

Chaco Canyon

Mysterious lines crisscross the dry, treeless landscape of northwestern New Mexico. Aerial photographs confirm that there is a pattern of lines—or roads— leading to various ancient Indian ruins.

Twelve large villages, or pueblos, of the ancient Anasazi people lie in ruin along the dry river bed of a region known as Chaco Canyon. The largest of its buildings is called Pueblo Bonito, a Spanish name that means "beautiful town." This thousand-year-old building has 800 rooms and many underground ceremonial chambers, or kivas. It was constructed of stone and built four stories tall. The building, in the shape of the letter "D", curves around a central courtyard where the Anasazi held their religious ceremonies.

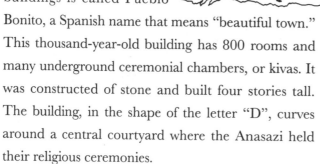

People who lived in ancient times seemed to know how to set the angle of their buildings to get the most benefit from the sun at different times of the year. Pueblo Bonito was built against the high stone walls of Chaco Canyon. Here it could reflect the heat of the summer and get the most warmth from the weaker winter sun.

Various styles of stone construction were used to build Pueblo Bonito. Archaeologists have studied these stone patterns to learn how the buildings were made and why certain styles of stonework were used. In 1947, part of the high cliff above Pueblo Bonito came crashing down with tons of rock that smashed through the walls and houses, destroying a section of the building. Huge boulders broke through the architecture and damaged some of the fine Anasazi stonework.

The lines of roads that seem to run in many different directions throughout Chaco Canyon remain a mystery. Most of the roads appear to be straight lines that cut across the landscape. At least 80 different villages in the Chaco region are connected by this strange system of roads.

Many ideas have been suggested as to why the roads were built. The roads may have been used as highways by people traveling to places of worship in the canyon. Some think the straight lines of the roads were used to sight certain stars or planets. It's also possible that the roads were built to make travel easier for merchants trading turquoise with Mexico.

Much more study needs to be done before we can learn the true purpose of the mysterious highways in Chaco Canyon.

This Anasazi village was once so pretty that Spanish explorers named it "beautiful town."

Casa Grande

In the desert of southern Arizona, a large building made of mud blocks stands like a giant box in the middle of a deserted village. Who constructed this strange building? What was its purpose, and when was it made?

More than 1,000 years ago, groups of people we call the "Hohokam" settled in the American Southwest. Their name means "Those Who Have Gone Before." The Hohokam were people who gave up fishing, and gathering to settle in the desert as farmers. They found ways to dig canals that would bring water from nearby rivers into the fields they planted with corn, beans, and squash.

As farmers, the Hohokam needed to know when the rains would come to the desert. They soon learned to "read the heavens" and record the seasons by observing the movements of the sun, moon, and stars. To do this properly, they constructed a five-story building with openings in the walls through which they could observe patterns of movement in the heavens.

Hundreds of years ago, the Hohokam vanished—and no one knows why. Many years after the great observatory of the Hohokam had fallen into ruin, Spanish explorers saw the remains of the building and called it Casa Grande, or "Big House."

Archaeologists in this century have examined this mysterious structure and have found some interesting features. Each side of the building faces one of the four main points of the compass—north, east, south, or west. Openings in the walls may be used to observe positions of the sun, moon, and stars at certain times of the year. The ancient astronomers who recorded this information learned to predict when the rainy season would come. They could then tell the farmers the best time to plant their crops and irrigate their fields.

Casa Grande was built of adobe, a material made by mixing mud with straw. This mixture is then shaped into blocks and baked in the sun. Over a period of time, rain can turn adobe blocks into mud again. Many adobe buildings in Hohokam villages have been ruined because they were not protected from the rains. Parts of Casa Grande also have been damaged by rain and wind.

Today Casa Grande is protected from rain by a large canopy that covers the building. This means that Casa Grande will be preserved for archaeologists who want to discover more of its mysteries—and for you to see if you visit.

Now protected by a canopy, this large building holds clues to early Native American life.

The Great Serpent Mound

The quarter-mile-long snake curving across the Ohio landscape appears to be swallowing an egg. This strange earthen construction was created more than a thousand years ago by the Adena people, one of several Eastern Woodland Indian tribes.

Some scientists think that the shape of a snake about to swallow an egg may refer to an eclipse of the sun. In stories told by the Indians, the snake represented the earth, and during an eclipse it appeared to be swallowing the sun. No one can be sure why the Great Serpent Mound was built, but it may have had something to do with the worship of the spirit world that was common among the Eastern Woodland Indians.

The great serpent mound in Ohio is one of several different types of earthworks constructed by the Adena Indians. The Adena, the Hopewell, and the Mississippian tribes were known as the Mound Builders. These Indian groups built earthworks that may be found throughout the eastern and midwestern United States.

The Mound Builders also built temple mounds and burial mounds. Most temple mounds were small pyramids of packed earth with flat tops. A temple for worship made of wood and straw stood on the flat top of the earthen pyramid. Burial mounds were dome-shaped, with a burial chamber inside the mound. Another type of earthwork took the form of a wall or circular enclosure. Earthworks of this type were found around sacred areas.

To build these great earthworks, people had to carry dirt in baskets to the mound-building site. They then packed the earth by stamping it with their feet. Others had to see that plans and designs were being followed. There also had to be enough food for the workers building the mound. The leaders of the people had to make sure that all the work was being done properly.

The many designs and shapes of the earthworks had special meanings for the Adena, the Hopewell, and the Mississippian tribes. But archaeologists have not yet been able to explain why all of the mounds were built, or what they meant to these ancient Indian peoples.

Amid the forest, a Native American people shaped this winding mound of earth.

The Great Medicine Wheel

On high ground throughout North America, arrangements of stones called medicine wheels can be found. Scientists are just beginning to discover their meaning. Medicine wheels vary in size, but they do have similar shapes. They look like wagon wheels lying on the ground. These patterns are almost always made by arranging small stones to form the shape of the wheel. There is a hub in the center, and spokes lead from the hub to the rim of the wheel. Piles of stones called cairns may be found at points along the rim of the wheel.

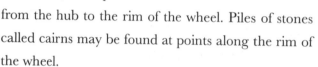

Most scientists now believe that the so-called medicine wheels were created by Indians living in North America about a thousand years ago. Medicine wheels may have been used as astronomical observatories. One very large medicine wheel, 82 feet in diameter, is located high in the Bighorn Mountains of Wyoming. The Indians in this area were hunters, and the medicine wheel appears to have served them as a hunting calendar. By looking along certain lines of sight from the stone cairns around the rim of the medicine wheel, the position of the sun and stars can be tracked to provide a hunter with valuable information. Sighting the summer solstice on June 21 allowed the Plains Indians to mark the beginning of summer. This was a time when the bison would begin to move into areas where they could be hunted.

Another interesting feature of the medicine wheel in Wyoming is the way in which it marks the summer months for hunting in the Bighorn Mountains. Sightings from the cairns across the spokes of the wheel can mark the position of certain stars. When the star of Aldebaran is sighted just before sunrise, a hunter knows that it is safe to go into the mountain because the snows are melting. When the star Rigel is sighted, the hunter is safe because it is the middle of the summer season. However, when the star Sirius appears along the sighting lines of the medicine wheel, it signals the hunter to leave the mountains before he is trapped by a snowfall.

The medicine wheel is just one example of how ancient peoples learned to chart the heavens. By searching the skies and recording their observations in great stone circles, they were better able to live in harmony with their environment.

This arrangement of stones may have been used as a calendar by Native American hunters.

The Great Zimbabwe

The mysteries of the Great Zimbabwe have challenged archaeologists for many years. Who built the stone walls and towers of this ancient city in Africa? What was the purpose of its elaborate architecture? When was the city built, and who built it? Why was it abandoned?

The ruins are located in the African nation formerly called Rhodesia, now called Zimbabwe. The archaeological site is called the Great Zimbabwe. The ruins are a series of stone towers and enclosures that first came to world attention in 1871.

Early explorers thought that the stone structures might be the work of Egyptians or other people who had a tradition of stoneworking. In the twentieth century, the large buildings, walls, and towers were shown to have been constructed by native African people between 1200 and 1500 A.D.

Riches that came from trade seem to be the reason for building the temples, towers and walls. Residents of the Great Zimbabwe became active in the trade and transport of gold from nearby mines to ports along the east coast of Africa. The Great Zimbabwe appears to have been designed to impress people with the wealth and power held by the leaders of the community. There is little evidence that it was constructed for military defense.

The Great Zimbabwe also may have been a religious center. Religious leaders of the community took part in ceremonies to help farmers grow crops and raise cattle. Walled cattle pens and cattle bones excavated at the site show the importance of cattle as food for the people of the Great Zimbabwe.

Archaeologists are very interested in why a society or civilization, after reaching a peak of greatness, begins to collapse and is eventually abandoned. If we can learn how this happens, we may be able to avoid the problems that caused past civilizations to fall into ruin. At the Great Zimbabwe there is evidence that cattle may have overgrazed the land, that people killed all of the game, that too much of the forest was cut for firewood, and that the people lost control of the trade routes that brought them wealth. When people let this happen, their eventual collapse is assured.

By the sixteenth century A.D., the Great Zimbabwe had been abandoned and left in ruin. Its crumbled walls, towers, and temples remain as the only reminder of its glorious past.

Now in ruins, this stone wall was once part of an important empire in eastern Africa.

The City of Manaus

A boat follows the twisted course of the Amazon River for 1,000 miles into the dense jungles of Brazil. Upon reaching the river port of Manaus, a strange sight appears. There, in the middle of the Amazon jungle, stands a large, elaborately decorated opera house. Famous singing stars from Europe have been paid enormous sums of money to make the long journey up the Amazon River to perform at this opera house.

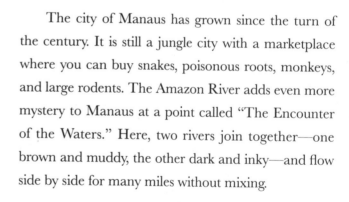

Many became ill with malaria and other diseases or even died after they entered this jungle environment.

The opera house came into this strange setting when rubber trees were discovered in the Amazon in the early twentieth century. Automobiles were just becoming popular, and this new means of transportation needed rubber tires. As the demand for rubber increased, the owners of the rubber plantations became wealthy. Isolated from European culture in the Brazilian jungles, the plantation owners thought that an opera house would be wonderful entertainment. With their great wealth, they built an ornate theater with unusual wood carvings, iron grills, and magnificent lights.

When someone smuggled the seeds of Brazilian rubber trees into Southeast Asia, plantation owners in the Amazon were no longer the only rubber suppliers in the world. Their fortunes declined, and their opera house was eaten by termites. After the opera house fell into ruins, the Brazilian government decided to restore this landmark in the jungle. Today it once again looks like the building that the rubber plantation owners built nearly a hundred years ago.

The city of Manaus has grown since the turn of the century. It is still a jungle city with a marketplace where you can buy snakes, poisonous roots, monkeys, and large rodents. The Amazon River adds even more mystery to Manaus at a point called "The Encounter of the Waters." Here, two rivers join together—one brown and muddy, the other dark and inky—and flow side by side for many miles without mixing.

The opera house, the marketplace, and the Encounter of the Waters are unique sights that make this Amazon jungle city a place of surprise and mystery.

This opera house was built by wealthy Europeans in a remote spot along the Amazon River.

Delphi

A temple, a stadium, a theater, treasury buildings, and a marketplace with fountains once stretched along a mountainside to form the spectacular sanctuary known in the ancient Greek world as Delphi. People from all over the Mediterranean world came here to take part in the games, the theater, and the worship of the Greek god Apollo.

Delphi had a stadium high on the mountainside where athletes competed in games. The seats of the spectators can still be seen along the starting gates where the foot races began. Just below the stadium, the seating area and stage of a large theater have been carved out of the mountain. Here plays were given to entertain the many pilgrims who came to the sanctuary of Apollo. On a ledge below the theater stood the great Temple of Apollo, where now only a few columns and foundation stones remain.

Many came to this place in the mountains of Greece to consult the oracle. The oracle was a woman who had been given the power of prophecy. She received visitors from her seat in the sacred temple, where she had visions that let her see into the future. Those who visited the oracle asked questions, and were given answers that could have two meanings. A king who asked what would happen if he made war on his enemy was told that a great empire would fall. Thinking that this meant his enemy would be defeated, he went to war. When he was defeated, the empire that fell was his own. The message of the oracle could always be interpreted in two ways.

This once-sacred site, today a jumble of fallen columns and carved stones, clings to the sloping mountain landscape. The main section of the sanctuary looks down on a deep valley where olive trees now grow. The view from Delphi looking out at the mountainous landscape is spectacular.

The sayings of the oracle, the procession of worshipers walking along the sacred way to the Temple of Apollo, and the many statues and buildings that once lined the paths are all part of the mystery of this sacred site.

At Delphi, visitors can see the Temple of Apollo where the Oracle made her predictions.

The Parthenon

Its mystery lies in its mathematics. The Parthenon of Athens, built to honor a goddess of wisdom, is considered to be the most perfect building in the history of western architecture.

Built as a temple to house a statue of the Greek goddess Athena, the Parthenon's architectural perfection was a way to honor the goddess. The Parthenon stands on the Acropolis, a rocky hill in the center of the ancient city of Athens. Originally a fortified area, the Acropolis became a sacred place where its temples would be on view for the people of Athens.

To construct a building that would please the goddess Athena, the ancient Greek architects planned a structure that would look perfect to the eye. To do this, they would have to use optical illusions and unusual proportions to fool the eye.

When seen against the sky, columns at the corners of a building look thinner than the other columns. Knowing this, the architects made the end columns of the Parthenon thicker so they would appear to be the same size as the rest of the columns.

They also made the middle of each column slightly thicker than the rest of the column. If the columns were the same thickness at the top, middle, and bottom, the middle section would look thinner and the column would not appear to be perfectly straight. Another unusual feature of the Parthenon is that all the columns lean slightly toward the center of the building. The entire structure is curved, because the building is higher in the center than it is at the sides. With these unusual proportions, you would think that there is not a straight line anywhere in the Parthenon. However, by using optical tricks and illusions, the architects of the Parthenon have made every line in the building look straight and perfectly balanced.

The most interesting mystery in the mathematics of the Parthenon is the proportion used by architects called The Golden Section Ratio. This ratio is found in things that grow in nature, such as seashells, plants, flowers, and trees. Many sections of the Parthenon follow these same proportions. By using mathematical secrets of the natural world, the ancient Greeks gave Athena a perfect home, and they gave the rest of the world a perfect building to copy.

Built to honor a goddess, the Parthenon is based on precise mathematical formulas.

The Gateway of the Sun

Life around Lake Titicaca, high in the Andes Mountains of Bolivia, has changed very little in the 2,000 years since the civilization of Tiahuanaco was established near its shores.

Fishermen in reed boats still cast their nets in the lake, and llamas carry goods to markets set up on the high plain that surrounds the lake. The Altiplano, as this region is called, stands 13,000 feet above sea level. Trees do not grow at this altitude, and there is little oxygen to support a fire. People who live here develop extra red blood cells to survive in the thin air. This unusual environment did not prevent ancient tribes from building cities and shrines on the Altiplano.

One of the most significant monuments at Tiahuanaco is called the Gateway of the Sun. The upper section of this huge block of stone is carved with a number of strange figures. The figure standing in the center of the gateway, just above the door, is believed to be the creator God, Viracocha. Figures with human heads and bird heads appear to be running toward Viracocha. The running figures all have wings with feathers made of bird heads, and they all seem to be carrying a staff or a scepter. Figures carved along the top of the gateway are thought to be a code for a calendar of 12 months of 30 days, or 36 weeks with a ten-day period in each week.

The fine carving of the figures on the Gateway of the Sun suggests that they were not meant for public view. This gateway may have been the entrance to a temple reserved for a special group of people. It's possible that Tiahuanaco was a religious shrine where ceremonies associated with certain calendar days took place. Tiahuanaco also could have been a pilgrimage site where people came for festivals and worship.

It was once thought that Tiahuanaco was a place of pilgrimage because the land around it was not very fertile and could not support a large permanent population. Archaeologists, however, have discovered large food-growing areas nearby. This new information could change the way we think about this mysterious place high in the Bolivian Andes of South America.

The sun, shown here through the Gateway to the Sun, was sacred to many ancient peoples.

The Pyramid of the Sun

When the Aztecs entered the Central Valley of Mexico in the thirteenth century, they discovered the ruins of a lost city. Even in ruin, the city impressed the new arrivals. The buildings looked too big to have been made by ordinary human beings. The Aztecs also thought that the bones of very large animals found nearby were the remains of giants who had built the city. Thinking that the giants were gods, the Aztecs called the city Teotihuacan (pronounced Tay-oh-tee-WHA-khan), which means "Home of the Gods."

The largest building in this ancient city is called the Pyramid of the Sun. Built over a small cave, this gigantic structure rises in four large terraces to a flat top where the remains of a temple can be seen. A broad stairway on the western side of the pyramid leads up to the temple.

Many archaeologists are convinced that the temple was related to the worship of the sun. A gold disc is said to have been placed on the eastern side of the temple, where it would have caught the first rays of the rising sun to announce the beginning of a new day.

The Pyramid of the Sun also appears to be a marker to measure the position of the sun at different times of the year. The ancient astronomers of Teotihuacan had stations where they could watch the sun rise over different sides of the pyramid at various times of the year. From their observations, the astronomers were able to tell the farmers when the rainy season would begin and when to plant their crops.

Archaeologists have studied the Pyramid of the Sun for nearly 100 years. Many of its secrets have not yet been revealed. We would like to know more about the people who built the pyramid, how they used it, and what it must have looked like when it was first finished. Early excavations were not well done, and parts of the pyramid were destroyed. New methods for doing archaeology may answer some of the important questions about the Pyramid of the Sun and the City of Teotihuacan.

From atop the pyramids, Mexican priests studied the heavens and predicted seasonal changes.

The Temple of the Thousand Masks

In the jungles of the Yucatan Peninsula of Mexico, a Maya temple built more than 1,000 years ago stands out as a cry for rain in a dry land. The Maya people worshiped a rain god whom they called Chac. This force that caused the life-giving rain to fall hid behind a mask that represented his presence in the land.

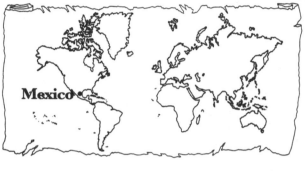

The mask of Chac has certain features that the Maya people understood. His large circle eyes represent drops of rainwater that fall from the sky. On his upper lip he wears a long curving mustache that was seen as the shape of a rain cloud. The teeth below look like the rain falling from the clouds. Small circles that are part of the Maya word for water decorate the eyelids of his mask. The long nose of Chac looks like half of the raincloud form set into the face of the mask.

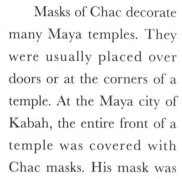

Masks of Chac decorate many Maya temples. They were usually placed over doors or at the corners of a temple. At the Maya city of Kabah, the entire front of a temple was covered with Chac masks. His mask was set along the length of the building from ground level to the top of the temple roof. Why so many masks on one building? The answer might be related to a drought that had come to the area. If the people had become desperate for rain, crops in the field were burning in the hot sun, and the earth had turned into a dry powder, Chac would have seemed to be ignoring the people's plea for rain.

The Temple of the Thousand Masks that the Maya built at Kabah was an attempt to win the favor of Chac by displaying his face over the entire surface of the building. This was to be the place where the Maya priests could make offerings to Chac that the rain god would hear.

Today this temple stands in ruin. Many of the masks of Chac have fallen from the temple, and their pieces lie scattered on the ground. Each year the summer rains fall on the ruins.

Stone carvings of the Maya god Chac may have been made as a desperate plea for rain.

The Cave of Balancanche

The Cave of Balancanche in the Yucatan Peninsula of Mexico contains many mysteries. The slippery rocks that lie at the entrance to the cave present a danger to explorers who descend into the depths of its endless caverns. A long, sloping path leads downward into vast underground spaces. Tree roots from the ground above have pushed through the ceiling of the cave and hang there like giant stalactites. As spaces begin to narrow, you must crawl on your hands and knees to pass through small tunnels into the next open space.

 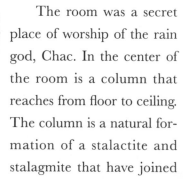

One of the great mysteries of the Cave of Balancanche was revealed in the middle of this century, when some hand-cut stones were removed from the base of a wall deep within the cave. This opened the entrance to a narrow passageway that had been sealed for nearly 1,000 years. The passageway led into a large circular room filled with Maya artifacts.

The room was a secret place of worship of the rain god, Chac. In the center of the room is a column that reaches from floor to ceiling. The column is a natural formation of a stalactite and stalagmite that have joined together. To the Maya, this stone column may have been seen as a sacred tree of life fed by the waters in the cave. All around the column, Maya worshipers had placed clay incense pots with the face of Chac.

Another surprise was the discovery of a small opening in the wall of the large circular room. This led down to the sandy shore of an underground lake. A small pottery vessel representing Chac stood on a platform in the middle of the shallow lake. Worshipers had placed rows of miniature corn-grinding stones along the shores of this deep underground lake. These stones were part of Maya ceremonies that asked Chac to send the life-giving rains that make the corn grow.

The Cave of Balancanche is of great interest to those who are trying to solve some of the mysteries of the ancient Maya.

Clay incense pots found in a cave suggest that this was a secret place of worship.

The Well of Sacrifice

Millions of years ago, countless shellfish swarmed in the ancient sea beds. As they died and sank to the bottom of the sea, their tiny shells were compressed into limestone. Earthquakes and volcanoes later pushed great masses of this limestone up to the surface of the earth. The Yucatan Peninsula of Mexico was formed in this way.

Water soaking through the limestone surface carved out tunnels and caves that formed a chain of underground rivers. In some places, these underground waters broke through the surface and left an opening in the earth. Water was often seen at the bottom of one of these natural wells, which the ancient Maya called a cenote.

One of the most important centers for the worship of the Maya rain god, Chac, was the Cenote of Sacrifice, located in the ancient city of Chichén Itzá in the heart of the Yucatan Peninsula.

The Cenote of Sacrifice is a natural, circular-shaped well 80 feet deep. Water at the bottom of the cenote was believed to be the home of Chac, and the well became a place to make offerings to the rain god. People came from many parts of the Maya region to drop bells, clay figures, jade objects, and carved bones into the well as they asked Chac to bring rain to their crops.

There are stories of Maya priests sacrificing young women to Chac by throwing them into the sacred well. If these stories are true, the bones of the sacrificial victims would be found in the well. But these stories of human sacrifice are not supported by evidence excavated from beneath the waters of the cenote.

The sacred cenote at Chichén Itzá must have been an important place of worship for the Maya people. Excavations of the cenote have uncovered many artifacts that tell us about Maya customs and beliefs.

Many people living in the Yucatan Peninsula today still get their water from cenotes found throughout the region, and they also continue to share the beliefs of their ancient ancestors.

96

Visitors to this natural well can only imagine the importance that it held for the Maya.

Mont-Saint-Michel

Violent storms and high tides caused a piece of land to break away from the coast of France more than 1,000 years ago. The island formed in this way, known today as Mont-Saint-Michel, became one of the most sacred places in medieval Europe.

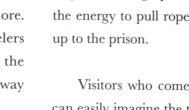

Pilgrims came from many countries to worship in the church that was built on top of the rocky hill of the island. To reach the church, people had to walk across the sand banks that separated the island from the mainland shore. These shifting sands were soft, and some travelers who became stuck in the sand drowned when the tide came in. In the nineteenth century, a causeway was built to connect the island with the mainland.

The monks who lived on the island during the Middle Ages added many new buildings to their original living quarters. In the fifteenth century, a new church was built on top of the older buildings, giving all the structures the shape of a giant pyramid.

Later, wars raging in Europe made it necessary to fortify the island. Walls began to encircle the buildings around the base of the church. To reach the long stairs that led up to the abbey, visitors had to pass through three sets of fortified gates.

When the French Revolution began in 1789, the buildings were used as a prison. Heavy gates, towers, and fortified walls enclosed dungeon-like rooms that became a prison. Workers assigned to walk inside a huge wheel cage placed high on the wall provided the energy to pull ropes that lifted food and supplies up to the prison.

Visitors who come to Mont-Saint-Michel today can easily imagine the time when Viking ships raided the island and pilgrims carefully crossed the tidal sands to reach this place of worship. The abbey seems filled with memories of monks climbing long flights of stairs to reach their church, and of prisoners looking out at the southwest coast of France through the narrow windows of their dungeon cells. However, it is the beauty of this sacred place, rising from the rock surrounded by tidal waters, that provides the most lasting memory of Mont-Saint-Michel.

Worshipers once risked their lives to reach this island cathedral.

The Sainte-Chapelle

The stained glass of this chapel in Paris is one of the most beautiful sights in Europe. This magnificent glass and stone structure was ordered in the thirteenth century by the king of France to keep a sacred treasure that was to be brought from the Holy Land.

At that time, Europeans kept holy relics in small decorated boxes that look like miniature buildings. The architects of the chapel had the task of creating a building that would look like one of these jewel boxes.

Ste. Chapelle was built in the Gothic style that was becoming popular in medieval Europe, with pointed arches, circular windows, and stone supports called buttresses. The architects made Ste. Chappelle into a Gothic glass box by setting 15 tall, stained-glass windows around the chapel and a huge circular window, or rose window, above the front door. From inside the chapel, this stained-glass rose window looks like a brightly colored flower in full bloom.

If you visit this chapel, you will enter through a lower chapel with a low ceiling. A narrow, spiral stone staircase leads from the lower chapel to the larger upper chapel. Here the 15 stained-glass windows soar upward, flooding the chapel with light. Inside, you are surrounded by colorful windows that contain some of the finest stained glass ever manufactured in Europe.

The Rose Window of Sainte-Chapelle

In the Middle Ages, few people could read or write. The stained-glass windows in churches told stories from the Bible, and every shape and design had meaning. The Rose Window was no exception. A rose is a symbol for the Virgin Mary, and a circle, which has no beginning and no end, is a symbol for eternity.

The patterns of this stained-glass window curl and intertwine with rich colors that make it glow like a jewel.

Built to look like a jewel box, this colorful chapel is lined with stained-glass windows.

Chimayo

Dozens of crutches hang from the walls of a church near Santa Fe, New Mexico, where people with illness and injuries come to be cured. The mission-style Church of Chimayo has become a major pilgrimage site for people throughout the southwestern United States.

The Sanctuary of Chimayo, built in the early nineteenth century, is associated with many stories of miracles. The person who built the church, Don Bernardo Abeyta, had a vision in which he was told that if he dug earth from a special place and rubbed it on his body, his illness would be cured. When this happened, he built a church over the hole where he had dug the earth.

Soon the sanctuary became famous, and people began to visit the site, hoping to find a cure for their illness by rubbing a bit of dirt on their bodies. In a side room of the church, discarded crutches and braces hang on the walls. Photographs, dolls, and notes of thanks fill the room where those cured of an illness after visiting the church have left behind memories of their experience.

The Sanctuary of Chimayo is located in a region that was once so far removed from civilization that it became a place to send people who had committed serious crimes. Today it has many visitors who come to see its picturesque architecture and the beautiful folk art that decorates the main altar of the church.

Those who come seeking a cure or who come to worship at this sacred place often walk many miles through a dry, hilly, desert-like landscape to reach the sanctuary. The mystery of this place is still a very powerful force in drawing pilgrims to this sacred shrine in the mountains of New Mexico.

Many stories of miracles surround this church, and many people come here to be healed.

The Old New Synagogue

More than a thousand years ago, Jewish families settled in the city of Prague, in Czechoslovakia. Sometimes the Jewish people prospered under the privileges they received from various kings, and they developed science, mathematics, book printing, music, and other arts. However, some kings were cruel to the Jews, and restricted them to certain areas of the city, called ghettos. Because the Jewish people did not

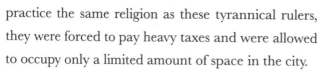

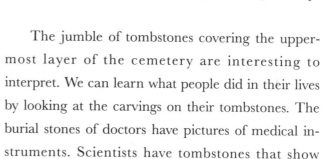

practice the same religion as these tyrannical rulers, they were forced to pay heavy taxes and were allowed to occupy only a limited amount of space in the city.

In the thirteenth century, members of the Jewish community of Prague decided to build a synagogue as a place of worship. The strange name—Old New Synagogue—may have come from the sound of the Hebrew words "altenai-schul," meaning "synagogue on the condition of." The name referred to a legend that the stones used to build the Old New Synagogue were on loan from a temple in Jerusalem, to be returned "on the condition of" the reopening of the synagogue in Jerusalem someday.

One of the strangest sights of the Old New Synagogue is its cemetery. Here space was severely restricted, and once all of the burial ground was occupied by graves, it became necessary to cover the entire cemetery with a thick layer of earth and start building a new burial ground on top. Over the centuries, this process was repeated many times. Today, some areas of the cemetery are 12 layers deep.

The jumble of tombstones covering the uppermost layer of the cemetery are interesting to interpret. We can learn what people did in their lives by looking at the carvings on their tombstones. The burial stones of doctors have pictures of medical instruments. Scientists have tombstones that show scientific equipment.

The Old New Synagogue is one of the oldest places in the world where Jewish people continue to worship. Its history, and the information gathered from its many tombstones, can be read as a testimony to the struggle of the Jewish people in Eastern Europe.

This synagogue was built nearly 1,000 years ago in the style of a medieval church.

A Jurassic Boneyard

They were called terrible lizards. Millions of years ago, these strange creatures roamed the earth and then vanished, leaving many questions about their origin and their extinction.

Evidence of their presence is concentrated in an area of Colorado and Utah known today as the Dinosaur Triangle. A number of fossil beds have been discovered near the towns of Vernal and Price in Utah and near Grand Junction, Colorado. From the study of fossils at these sites, scientists hope to solve some of the mysteries of the dinosaurs.

At Vernal, Utah, a wall of sandstone in which dinosaurs lie has been enclosed in a glass building. Here scientists can work on the process of excavation without concern for the weather. The building also houses a laboratory next to the excavation site. Bones taken from the fossil bed can be delivered immediately to the lab for study and preservation.

The boneyard at Vernal is believed to have formed when dinosaurs that died 140 million years ago were washed down a river to a place where they became stuck in a sandbar. The bones buried in the sand were eventually covered by a mile-thick layer of mud and volcanic ash. Later, earthquakes and volcanic upheavals in this region pushed the fossil-bearing sandstone layers up to the surface of the earth. After millions of years of erosion had worn down the rock, the fossil layers were exposed and later discovered.

Visitors who come to the quarry at Vernal can walk along the rock wall where the dinosaur bones lie exposed and watch scientists in the process of excavating the bones. The building also offers a view of the laboratory where the bones are being studied.

The bones found at Vernal are those of dinosaurs that died long before the time when dinosaurs became extinct, 65 million years ago. Scientists at Vernal are looking at animals that lived in the middle of the dinosaur era near the end of the Jurassic period, about 140 million years ago.

The many different kinds of fossils found at Vernal give us a much clearer picture of how dinosaurs lived and what their world was like. This information will be of great value in understanding why certain animals are becoming extinct today, and what we can do to prevent this.

Studying fossils may help scientists discover why the dinosaurs disappeared.

Devil's Tower

The Kiowa Indians call it Mateo Tipi, or Grizzly Bear Lodge. Today this strange rock formation in northeastern Wyoming is called the Devil's Tower. Shaped like a giant tree trunk, this natural tower is 867 feet high, with a flat top that has an acre and a half of ground. The base is about 1,000 feet in diameter.

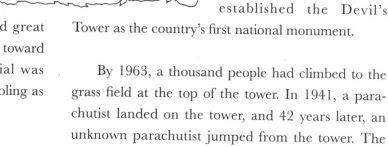

Sixty million years ago, as dinosaurs were becoming extinct, the earth was in a stage of upheaval. This was a time when the Rocky Mountains were rising out of the earth and great masses of molten rock were being pushed up toward the surface of the land. Super-hot material was squeezing through cracks in the earth and cooling as it rose toward the surface.

This process left unusual stone formations buried within the earth. These hardened volcanic materials were surrounded by softer rock layers, and over millions of years these layers eroded away, leaving the harder stone shapes standing above the landscape. The Devil's Tower was formed in this way.

Many visitors have been attracted to this mysterious stone shape at the western end of the Black Hills. The tower was first climbed in 1893. In 1906, U.S. President Theodore Roosevelt established the Devil's Tower as the country's first national monument.

By 1963, a thousand people had climbed to the grass field at the top of the tower. In 1941, a parachutist landed on the tower, and 42 years later, an unknown parachutist jumped from the tower. The tower also plays a featured role in the 1978 science-fiction film, *Close Encounters of the Third Kind*.

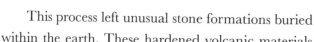

The Seven Sisters

Indians living near the Devil's Tower explained the giant stone formation through myth and legend. One story tells of seven Indian girls chased by bears, who escaped by jumping on a rock that suddenly rose up, lifting them to a height where the bears could no longer reach them.

As the bears scratched at the rock, the children were lifted to the heavens where they became the seven stars in the group we call the Pleiades.

This story explains why the outer layer of stone surrounding the Devil's Tower looks like the scratch marks of a giant bear. This layer of stone is actually made up of four-, five-, or six-sided columns of stone that formed when the hot volcanic material cooled and hardened.

This massive rock formation in Wyoming continues to capture people's imaginations.

Iguaçu Falls

The airplane slowly circles through the mist, and then plunges downward to give passengers a closeup view of one of the greatest waterfalls on earth. At Iguaçu Falls, the waters of the Parana River fall over steep rock cliffs with a thunderous roar to offer one of the most spectacular displays of raw power in nature. Located where the borders of Brazil, Argentina, and Paraguay meet in southern South America, Iguaçu

Falls is the earth's seventh largest waterfall by volume, and one of the great natural wonders of the world.

Nearly 300 waterfalls meet at Iguaçu to put on a show of rainbows and mists set against the background sounds of water crashing down from great heights. Colorful butterflies abound, and small birds called swifts dart in and out of the falls. The swifts live on the rocky cliffs under the falls, where they are safe from predators. The birds have learned to fly through the cascades so that they can raise their young behind a protective wall of water.

In the language of the Guarani Indians, who once lived near the falls, Iguaça means "Plenty of Water." When rains come to the Iguaçu region, however, the entire canyon of the Parana River is flooded by an enormous wall of water. The rush of water in one section of the falls is so fierce that it is known as the Devil's Throat.

In the 1700s, Jesuit missionaries came from Europe to this remote region of South America to establish communities with the Guarani Indians. For a while, they were rather successful in farming and raising cattle. Eventually, the missionaries were attacked and sent out of the country. The Indians returned to their native ways, and the mission buildings fell into ruins.

Today, people come from all parts of the world to settle in this fast-growing region, and to see one of nature's greatest waterfalls. Brazil, Argentina, and Paraguay have recognized the beauty and power of the magnificent waterfall that touches their borders, and all three countries have declared Iguaçu to be a protected area and public park.

Admired for centuries, this magnificent waterfall is now protected as part of a park.

Bryce Canyon

"It was a heck of a place to lose a cow!" said Ebenezer Bryce, an early settler in southwest Utah. It surely would be difficult to find a cow among the thousands of richly colored, tree-like stone columns and natural walls throughout Bryce Canyon.

Mr. Bryce did not seem to appreciate the great beauty of the unusual stone formations in the canyon that now bears his name, but thousands of visitors come to Bryce Canyon National Park each year to enjoy the spectacular display of the naturally carved stone formations.

Bryce Canyon was formed millions of years ago. Oceans once covered the area where Bryce Canyon is now located. Sand, mud, and rocks from mountains around the oceans washed into the waters of these seas. When these materials settled to the bottom, pressure packed them together into thick stone formations. Eventually, volcanic forces caused the oceans to drain away, and the land was pushed up, to a high point of nearly two miles. This massive stone formation that had been lifted from the bottom of the sea soon began to crack and split into sections that formed a series of step-like plateaus. Bryce Canyon was formed from one of these plateaus.

The many kinds of stone that had formed in layers on the ancient sea beds were now exposed on the cliff walls of the plateau. Water, wind, and snow began to carve these layered stone cliffs. Pressures that built up inside the plateau caused vertical cracks to form in the stone. Rainwater running into these cracks split them open, forming large spaces between the rocks. Ice formed in the cracks, and caused more of the rocks to split.

After millions of years of erosion, the stone spires and columns that give Bryce Canyon its unusual beauty began to take shape. Nature has carved the layers of stone into figures that look like people in costume, or animals in various poses. Erosion has formed natural bridges and walls with window-like openings. One tilted stone cliff looks like a sinking ship. Minerals in the layers of stone add beautiful colors to the strange shapes.

Today there are many places along the rim of Bryce Canyon where a visitor may stop and view the magnificent stone formations in a fantasy land of shapes and colors that delight the eye. It is easy to understand why the Indians called this place "Red rocks standing like men in a bowl-shaped canyon."

The strangely beautiful landscape of Bryce Canyon was created by erosion.

The Stone Wonders of Cappadocia

Millions of years ago, volcanoes erupted in central Turkey and created a strange landscape. Layers of ash and molten rock deposited by the volcanoes hardened into stone. As centuries of rain, wind, and snow eroded the stone, the landscape became transformed into a fantasy of unusual stone formations.

Today this region is known as Cappadocia. People who settled here in early times discovered that the odd rock formations were soft enough to be carved with hammers and chisels. Some people

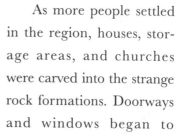

began to carve their houses into the rock cones that seemed to be everywhere. Others lived in natural caves that had been produced when pockets of air were trapped in the molten rock during the volcanic eruptions.

As more people settled in the region, houses, storage areas, and churches were carved into the strange rock formations. Doorways and windows began to appear in the huge cone-shaped stones. Some spaces carved out of the soft rock were decorated with paintings. In rooms that would serve as churches, walls were covered with plaster. While the plaster was still wet, artists painted scenes that illustrated stories from the Bible. When the plaster dried the paint dried with it, forming a type of painting known as fresco.

People lived in these unusual stone formations for more than 1,000 years. By the twentieth century, the living spaces carved out of the rock had begun to show wear—the result of continuous erosion—and the area was no longer safe. Walls developed dangerous cracks, and stone roofs began to crumble. By 1950, people living in the cone formations and in the natural caves of Cappadocia were forced to leave.

Today, the area is an abandoned, ghost-like place that invites the visitor to see a strange combination of natural and man-made wonders in stone.

These unusual stone formations were soft enough to be carved into cave dwellings.

Rainbow Bridge

Many seasoned explorers failed in their attempts to find the great "stone rainbow" that was said to lie hidden in remote regions of the American Southwest. Some Indians and a few prospectors had talked of seeing a great arch of stone in the 1800s.

When an expedition set out in 1909 to find the natural stone arch that we now call Rainbow Bridge, they met with great difficulties. The rugged landscape of weather-carved stone formations blocked their path, and large areas of steeply sloping, slippery rock were dangerous to cross. Not even the Indian guides who led the explorers on horseback deeper into the twisted canyons were sure where they were going.

With the feet of their horses cut and bleeding from the jagged rocks along the trail, the expedition leaders finally arrived at the soaring arch of Rainbow Bridge. At that time they were among the very few people ever to see this magnificent natural wonder.

Located in the southeastern corner of the state of Utah, Rainbow Bridge was formed millions of years ago by forces within the earth that pushed up large land masses. After this happened, water began to cut into the raised rock formations, carving out deep canyons in the region. Water trapped behind a stone formation slowly eroded the rock until it formed a hole through which it could flow. In time, water flowing through the hole in the rock enlarged the opening. Eventually, the rock formation took on the shape of an arched bridge.

In the background of Rainbow Bridge is the 10,000-foot-high Navajo Mountain. To the Navajo of the region, the mountain and the Rainbow Bridge are sacred places. The Navajo see the great stone arch as a rainbow, associated with rain clouds and the life-giving rainfall. The rain clouds that gather around the top of Navajo Mountain also are a reminder of the mystical, spiritual powers of water. Today Rainbow Bridge is a "rain-calling" site for Navajo people who come here to pray for rain.

The great natural stone arch called Rainbow Bridge is sacred to the Navaho people.

Yellowstone National Park

It was one of the most powerful explosions that ever shook the planet Earth. More than a half million years ago, lava from a huge volcano gushed out of the earth and covered a wide area of what is now western Wyoming. As molten lava poured out, the inside of the volcano emptied. Then, in a massive explosion, the entire volcano collapsed in on itself, creating a huge crater.

No one would believe the stories told in the mid-nineteenth century by trappers and mountain men who had explored this area. They spoke of geysers, pots of boiling mud, and rivers of hot water creating steam as they ran through the countryside. When scientific expeditions into the region confirmed these so-called wild stories, people became very interested in this fantastic place.

Today this region is known as Yellowstone National Park. In 1872, Yellowstone became the first national park in the United States. Its unusual features are the result of volcanic activity that is still going on in the park. In other places, geologists would have to drill five miles into the earth to reach the extreme heat and red-hot lava that lies less than 300 feet from the earth's surface at Yellowstone.

One feature of the park that is not very well known to visitors is a mountain of glass. This glass, called obsidian, was used by the Indians of the region to make tools and weapons.

For the many visitors who come to Yellowstone each year, it is the geysers, bubbling mud pots, and brightly-colored hot-water pools that provide the main attraction. The most famous geyser is known as "Old Faithful," because it faithfully erupts every hour, to the delight and amazement of visitors.

To the Indians who roamed this region of Yellowstone, these wonders of nature inspired fear and respect. But it was the mysterious glass mountain, the source of the magical material called obsidian, that attracted prehistoric visitors to the Yellowstone region many thousands of years ago.

The Black Glass Mountain

Obsidian is a black, volcanic glass that is easy to chip or flake.

Using large bones or sections of reindeer antlers, the Indians who lived in what is now Wyoming struck chunks of raw obsidian, breaking it into pieces that they then shaped into knife blades and spear points.

The volcanic activity of Yellowstone provided the Indians with a mountain of obsidian.

Towers of water shooting out of the ground show volcanic activity still taking place.

The Craters of the Moon

In the northwestern United States, there is a place so forbidding that the region was not explored until this century. Volcanic eruptions 15,000 years ago formed a mysterious landscape of cinder cones and tubes in the region of Idaho now called Craters of the Moon National Monument.

Those who first crossed these lava fields experienced great hardship. The lava rocks cut their shoes, and they had to carry lots of water with them. Temperatures in this area can rise to more than 150 degrees. The black lava rock does not reflect the heat of the sun, so the temperature stays very high. Plant life is scarce, because water quickly evaporates in the heat, and vegetation dies from lack of moisture.

Trails have now been built to allow visitors to explore the volcanic formations that make up the strange landscape of this national park. Here rivers of molten lava that have hardened into ribbons of black stone lie silent among the hills. In some areas, lava fragments called bombs can be seen scattered over the ground. These are chunks of lava that exploded from eruptions and cooled and hardened in the air before they fell to earth. Lava flowing over trees took the shape of the tree bark to form some unusual stone surfaces. Other lava formations are rugged enough to tear holes in a hiker's boot.

Long tubes of lava formed when molten rock cooled to form a crust that hardened on the outside, yet allowed the hotter molten rock within to drain out, leaving a tunnel of lava. Stalactites of lava or ice that formed within the tubes add to their strange beauty.

Cinder cones that look like flat-topped hills were formed when eruptions threw out cinders that piled up around the crater from which they were ejected. Spatter cones were formed when a sticky form of lava was thrown out in a volcanic eruption. This material stuck to other stones and formed cone shapes.

To walk through this fantastic landscape of lava tubes, cinder cones, and spatter cones is to see the earth as it may have looked on the eve of creation.

This unearthly place is in Idaho—and it's now part of a national park.

Pamukkule

At the top of a mountain, hot water containing rich mineral substances from deep within the earth gushes from a spring and forms a series of gleaming terraces before it flows into the valley below. This natural wonder in central Turkey must be seen to be believed. As the water cascades down the mountainside, it constantly deposits lime along the ledges of the mountain slope. The lime accumulates and hardens to form terraces that hold pools of water. As water flows over an upper terrace, the lime it contains begins to form a new terrace wall that will fill with a pool of water. Over many centuries, this process has created a step-like pattern of bright, white terraces that appear to climb the mountainside. Pools of blue-green water fill the terraces and spill over them in a magnificent cascade. In Turkey this sight is called Pamukkule, which means "cotton castles."

In ancient times the Romans built the city of Hierapolis at Pamukkule and used this natural hot-water spring in their bathhouses. They believed that bathing in these waters could cure certain illnesses and diseases. People still come from all over the world to bathe in the pools of water that collect behind the terraces. At the bottom of the pools, deposits of lime that have not yet hardened are scooped up by bathers who smear their bodies with it, perhaps believing that the minerals in the water have healing properties.

Unusual formations of lime-formed terraces may also be seen in the United States in the heart of Yellowstone Park, in Wyoming. At a site called Mamouth Hot Springs, lime-laden waters have formed a series of terraces that look very much like those at Pamukkule. At Mamouth Hot Springs, no one is allowed to bathe in the pools of water that collect behind the terraces. This wonder of nature is being preserved for future generations to see.

Limestone pools like this are located in central Turkey and in Yellowstone National Park.

The Florissant Fossil Beds

Butterflies, tiny insects, and giant redwood trees trapped by the ash of erupting volcanoes—all were turned to stone. When this happened, 35 million years ago in the heart of Colorado, the Florissant Fossil Beds were born.

Volcanic activity can preserve small insects as well as giant redwood trees. In some cases, a fine ash thrown into the air by volcanoes covered insects and buried them in layers of mud that later hardened into rock. This preserved many different types of insects that lived 35 million years ago. The Florissant Fossil Beds became one of the few areas in the world where scientists could find insects so well preserved.

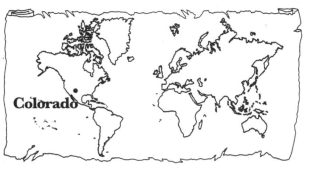

The volcanic eruptions in this region also started mudflows that rolled over the earth toward a forest of giant redwood trees. The mud gathered around the base of the redwoods to a height of 15 feet. Stuck in this thick layer of mud, the trees began to die. As the treetops decayed, the lower parts that were covered with mud became fossilized. Minerals in the mud and water began to replace the cells of the wood, turning them to stone. The stone formed in this way looks exactly like the wood and bark of a living tree.

Scientists are very interested in the plant life seen in the fossil record at the Florissant Fossil Beds. Studies have shown that the warmer climate millions of years ago supported plants that could not grow in this region today. The ground level in this area was later pushed up by forces within the earth to a height of 8,400 feet—a mile higher than it was 35 million years ago, when the fossil beds were first being formed. This great uplift changed the types of plants that could grow at this higher altitude.

The plants and insects preserved at the Florissant Fossil Beds provide scientists with important information about living things that existed millions of years ago.

This is a good place to collect insects—especially ones that are 35 million years old.

The Grand Canyon

The Spanish explorers had come to a wide ridge that opened into a canyon below. They looked down at a miniature world of stone spires, and a tiny creek that flowed through the colorful stones of the unusual landscape. The sight before them could not be clearly understood. Without realizing where they were, some of the explorers began to descend into the canyon.

At about 1,000 feet below the rim of the canyon, they began to recognize their mistake. What they had seen from above was a mile-deep cut in the earth. What had appeared to be miniature spires were gigantic rocks, larger than the cathedrals of Spain. The tiny creek was a raging torrent of a river.

In 1640, the Spanish explorers had reached the rim of the Grand Canyon. At the time, they had no idea of the canyon's enormous size or depth. Exhausted from their thousand-foot descent, the explorers were still unaware that they would have to continue down another 4,000 feet into the canyon before they would reach the river at the bottom.

Today we have a much better understanding of this wonderful natural creation. Geologists have a great interest in the Grand Canyon because the Colorado River, which cuts the canyon one mile deep, has revealed some of the oldest rocks on earth. Rocks 500 million years old have been exposed at the bottom of the canyon as the river cuts deeper and deeper into the earth. Rocks in layers above these stone formations are from 120 to 190 million years old. In some areas, the canyon walls are a layer cake of geological stone formations that outline the history of the earth.

A study of these layers and the fossils in each level has given scientists information about the earliest forms of life on our planet. A band of a mineral called iridium occurs at a level that was laid down 60 million years ago. Iridium may have been introduced when thousands of meteors showered the earth, kicking up enormous clouds of dust that blotted out the sun and killed much of the plant life on earth. Some scientists think that this event led to the extinction of the dinosaurs.

Erosion in the canyon has created colorful stone formations of strange and unusual shapes. Minerals washing out of the rocks have created magnificent patterns of color.

More than a million and a half visitors come to enjoy the display of natural wonders at the Grand Canyon every year.

Viewed from the rim, it's hard to realize that this canyon is a mile deep.

The Running Press Start Exploring™ Series

Color Your World

With crayons, markers and imagination, you can re-create works of art and discover the worlds of science, nature, and literature.

Each book is $8.95 and is available from your local bookstore. If your bookstore does not have the volume you want, ask your bookseller to order it for you (or send a check/money order for the cost of each book plus $2.50 postage and handling to Running Press).

ARCHITECTURE

by Peter Dobrin

Tour 60 world-famous buildings around the world and learn their stories.

BULFINCH'S MYTHOLOGY

Retold by Steven Zorn

An excellent introduction to classical literature, with 16 tales of adventure.

FOLKTALES OF NATIVE AMERICANS

Retold by David Borgenicht

Traditional myths, tales, and legends, from more than 12 Native American peoples.

FORESTS

by Elizabeth Corning Dudley, Ph.D.

Winner, *Parents' Choice*
"Learning and Doing Award"

The first ecological coloring book, written by a respected botanist.

GRAY'S ANATOMY

by Fred Stark, Ph.D.

Winner, *Parents' Choice*
"Learning and Doing Award"

A voyage of discovery through the human body, based on the classic work.

INSECTS

by George S. Glenn, Jr.

Discover the secrets of familiar and more unusual insects.

MASTERPIECES

by Mary Martin and Steven Zorn

Line drawings and lively descriptions of 60 world-famous paintings and their artists.

MASTERPIECES OF AMERICAN ART

From the National Museum of American Art, Smithsonian Institution
by Alan Gartenhaus

Sixty ready-to-color masterpieces and their stories, including contemporary works.

OCEANS

by Diane M. Tyler and James C. Tyler, Ph.D.

Winner, *Parents' Choice*
"Learning and Doing Award"

An exploration of the life-giving seas, in expert text and 60 pictures.

SPACE

by Dennis Mammana

Share the discoveries of history's greatest space scientists and explorers.